THE
SUPER
DUPER
JOKE
BOOK

Volume 2

APPLESAUCE PRESS

KENNEBUNKPORT, MAINE

13-Digit ISBN: 978-1-60433-959-8
10-Digit ISBN: 1-60433-959-4

This book may be ordered by mail from the publisher. Please include $5.99 for postage and handling. Please support your local bookseller first!

Books published by Cider Mill Press Book Publishers are available at special discounts for bulk purchases in the United States by corporations, institutions, and other organizations. For more information, please contact the publisher.

Applesauce Press is an imprint of
Cider Mill Press Book Publishers
"Where good books are ready for press"
PO Box 454
12 Spring Street
Kennebunkport, Maine 04046
Visit us online! cidermillpress.com

Typography: Blast-O-Rama, Cherry Cream Soda, Cotran, Gill Sans, Handgypt, Jumping Bean, Litterbox, Oz Handicraft, Postino, Prater, Providence, Smilage

Printed in China
1 2 3 4 5 6 7 8 9 0
First Edition

CONTENTS

CHAPTER 1

MEDICAL MAYHEM

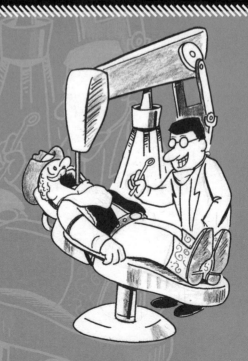

Why did the clothesline go to the hospital?
It had a knot in its stomach.

▶ ▶ ▶ ▶ ▶ ▶ ▶ ▶ ▶ ▶ ▶ ▶ ▶ ▶ ▶ ▶ ▶ ▶ ▶ ▶

Why did the clothesline go to the psychologist?
Its nerves were frayed.

◀ ◀ ◀ ◀ ◀ ◀ ◀ ◀ ◀ ◀ ◀

BETTER!

What did the monster eat after the dentist filled his sore tooth?
The dentist.

▶ ▶ ▶ ▶ ▶ ▶ ▶ ▶ ▶ ▶

Why did the sick shoe go to the cobbler?
It wanted to be heeled.

◀ ◀ ◀ ◀ ◀ ◀ ◀ ◀ ◀ ◀

A new patient went to see a doctor. "Who did you consult about your illness before you came to me?" asked the doctor. Said the patient, "I went to the pharmacist down the street." The man's reply angered the doctor who didn't like anyone but a physician giving out medical information. "And what idiotic advice did he give you?" snapped the doctor. Replied the patient softly, "He told me to come see you."

▶ ▶

Doctor: The pain in your left arm is caused by old age.
Patient: But Doc, my right arm is the same age and it doesn't hurt at all!

Patient: I'm depressed because everyone takes advantage of me.
Doctor: That's ridiculous. Don't give it another thought.
Patient: Thanks, Doc. I feel better now. How much do I owe you?
Doctor: How much do you have?

Why are surgeons good comedians?
They always have their audience in stitches.

◄ ◄ ◄ ◄ ◄ ◄ ◄ ◄ ◄ ◄ ◄ ◄ ◄ ◄ ◄ ◄

A hospital administrator was talking to a patient who demanded to be released. "Why did you jump up and run out of the operating room before your operation?" he asked the patient. "Because," the patient answered, "I heard the nurse say, 'Stop trembling and calm down. Be brave. This is just a simple operation.'"
"Didn't her words reassure you?"
"Heck no," said the patient, "she was talking to the surgeon."

Mad Doctor: Nurse! I see spots before my eyes.
Nurse: Relax. That's just the Invisible Man. He has the measles.

▶ ▶ ▶ ▶ ▶ ▶ ▶ ▶ ▶ ▶ ▶ ▶ ▶ ▶ ▶ ▶

Psychologist: You are not a pocket watch.
Patient: I want a second-hand opinion.

What kind of boat does a dentist ride on?
A tooth ferry.

Patient: Doc, you have to help me. I always feel like I'm on the outside looking in.
Psychiatrist: What kind of work do you do?
Patient: I'm a window cleaner.

Nurse: What should a patient do when he's run down?
Doctor: Get the license plate of the car.

Patient to their psychologist: You have to help me, Doc. I'm so depressed I have to wear a neck brace just to keep my chin up.

Girl: I wish the doctor would hurry up and see me. I'm only four years old.
Nurse: Be a little patient, dear.
Girl: I already am one!

Man: Doctor, my left ear feels hotter than my right ear. Is it an infection?
Doctor: No, your toupee is on crooked.

Mother: My son thinks he's a trash can.
Doctor: That's garbage.

Patient: Doc, am I really as ugly as people say I am?
Psychologist: Of course not.
Patient: Then why did you make me lie facedown on your couch?

Patient: What should I do if I can't sleep at night?
Doctor: Take naps all day long.

Lady: Doctor, my daughter thinks she's a sheet of music.
Psychologist: Bring her in and I'll take some notes.

Psychologist: I have a patient who thinks he's a taxicab.
Psychiatrist: Are you curing him?
Psychologist: Why should I? He drives me home every night.

Larry: I'm considering going to a psychologist.
Gary: What? Do you know how much that costs? You ought to have your head examined.

Where did the tin man go after he retired?
A rust home.

Patient: Help me, doctor! I just swallowed my harmonica.
Doctor: Luckily you don't play the piano.

Why did the actor end up at the hospital?
Everyone told him to break a leg.

Why did the miner go to a podiatrist?
He had coal feet.

Patient: Help me, doctor! I think I'm a bridge.
Doctor: My, my! What's come over you?
Patient: Two trucks and a minivan.

Patient: What do you mean I'm a hypochondriac?
Doctor: Your sickness is all in your mind.
Patient: Then refer me to a psychologist!

Show me a doctor who specializes in pelvic disorders and I'll show you a guy with a hip job.

A doctor was talking to a patient when his nurse burst into the room. "The patient you treated before this one just collapsed on his way out of the office. What should I do?" Replied the doctor calmly, "Turn him around so he looks like he collapsed on his way in."

What does a nurse call a sunburn emergency?
Code Red.

A lady went to see a psychologist. "Doctor," she said to him. "You have to help my husband. He just won the lottery and now all he does is worry about his money."

The doctor comforted the lady. "There! There!" he said. "Calm yourself. Send your husband to me and after a few months of therapy he won't have that problem anymore."

Nurse: Now the patient thinks he's a door.
Psychologist: Maybe he'll finally start opening up.

● ●

What did the patient say to the clumsy dentist?
You're getting on my nerves.

What did Dr. Oz tell the sick Tin Man?
Go home and get plenty of bed rust.

THIS DIAL INDICATES THAT YOU'RE RUNNING A TEMPERATURE!

Man: Doctor, I'm suffering from insomnia.
Doctor: That's a tough one. Let me sleep on it.

How did the nervous carpenter break his teeth?
He bit his nails.

Jack: Do you still have a bad case of sunburn?
Jill: Yes, but now I'm peeling better.

Patient: My hair is falling out.
What can you give me
to keep it in?
Doctor: How about a paper bag?

Man: Help me, Doc! My wife
thinks she's a pretzel.
Doctor: Bring her in and I'll
straighten her out.

ATTENTION: A doctor peers at charts while a dock tour charts piers.

Man: Every time I travel on a plane I get sick.
Doctor: It sounds like you have the flew.

Boy: If you broke your arm in two places,
what would you do?
Girl: Stay out of those two places.

Patient: Doc, how do you get rid of a pain
in the neck?
Doctor: Tell them to leave you alone.

TAKE TWO OF THESE AND DON'T CALL ME AGAIN!

A man went to his doctor for a checkup. After the exam the doctor gave the patient these instructions: "Take this blue pill with two glasses of water before breakfast," said the doctor. "Then before lunch take this red pill with three glasses of water. After dinner take this green pill with four glasses of water." The patient gulped. "Gee, Doc," he stammered. "This sounds serious. What's wrong with me?" The doctor answered, "You're not drinking enough water."

A Hollywood psycologist received a postcard from one of her famous starlet clients who was on vacation in the South Pacific. "I'm having a wonderful time," the starlet scribbled on the card. "I wish you were here to tell me why."

Why did Mr. & Mrs. Turtle take their son to a psychologist?
They couldn't get their son to come out of his shell.

Zack: Did you hear about the pig farmer who got swine flu?
Jack: No. What happened to her?
Zack: She went hog wild.

Kerry: Did you hear about the guy who broke his legs in a revolving door?
Jerry: No. Is he okay?
Kerry: Things are really turning around for him.

Why did the vampire take his son to the doctor?
He was eating necks to nothing.

Why did Frankenstein's monster go to the ER?
He was in shock.

Mo: My doctor is also a real estate agent.
Jo: They must make a lot of house calls.

Nurse: Why didn't the lady want the surgeon to operate on her husband?
Orderly: She didn't want anyone to open up her male.

What do you call a patient at a doctor's office?
Someone sick and tired of waiting.

Why did the baby rocket go to the doctor?
It was time for his booster.

Which doctor has the best voice?
The choirpractor.

Ben: My doctor told me to take a tranquilizer once a month.
Len: When?
Ben: Just before his bill arrives in the mail.

Doctor: Where does it hurt, Mr. Cherry?

Mr. Cherry: In the pit of my stomach.

Why did Santa Claus go to a psychologist?
Because he didn't believe in himself.

Chester: How's your Aunt Charlotte?

Lester: Her memory and her health are both failing her. She can't remember the last time she felt good.

What is a podiatrist's favorite TV game show?
Heel of fortune.

ATTENTION: Podiatrists never win. All they ever see is de feet.

**Why do prison wardens carry face wash?
It helps them prevent breakouts.**

What do you get if you cross a star and a podiatrist?
Twinkle toes.

Patient: Please help me, doctor. I honestly believe that people don't care about anything I have to say.

Psychologist: So what?

Patient: How can I cure my double vision quickly?
Doctor: Shut one eye.

Man: Doctor, can you cure my fear of needles?
Doctor: I can give it a shot.

Doctor: Don't you know my office hours are from nine to five and it's after five?
Patient: Yes, Doc, but the dog that bit me couldn't tell time.

Then there was the dentist who moved to Texas because he wanted to drill for oilmen.

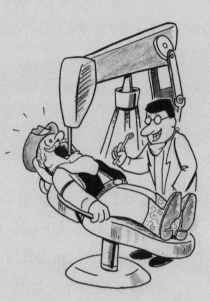

Psychologist: I'm happy to say that you are cured of your delusions, Mr. Johnson. But why are you so sad?
Mr. Johnson: Wouldn't you be sad if one day you were a Hollywood movie star, a famous war hero, and a pro football player, and the next day you were just an ordinary guy?

Minnie: How old is your grandfather?
Vinnie: He's at the age when all the numbers he knows are for doctors, nurses, and hospitals.

Ted: Did you hear about the rich hypochondriac?

Ed: No what about him?

Ted: He went around in a chauffeur-driven ambulance.

Man: I'm suing my employer because I got this bump on my head at work.

Lawyer: I bet we can get them to settle for a lump sum.

Where do phlebotomists go to college?
IV league schools.

Cop: Why did you jump in the icy river during the middle of a blizzard just to get your hat?

Man: Because if I go without a hat in this kind of weather, I always catch a cold.

ATTENTION: Pirate doctors will fix what sails you.

Why did the werewolf go to the psychologist?
He had a hair-raising experience.

Patient: Did you hear what I told you? I said I'm as sick as a dog!

Doctor: Stop barking at me and sit down.

Darla: Jenny got engaged to an x-ray technician.
Carla: I wonder what he sees in her?

Joe: If that were my sore tooth, I'd have it pulled.
Moe: If it were your sore tooth, I'd agree with you.

Did you hear about the boy who wanted to be a dentist?
He was enameled by the profession.

Why did the nice doctor go broke?
He never thought ill of anyone.

Why did the worm go to the doctor?
He was worried he'd catch bird flu.

Which famous pirate was a podiatrist?
Jean LaFeet.

Cora: I got airsick last week.
Lora: Were you in an airplane?
Cora: No. In Los Angeles.

Why do dentists never lie?
They value the tooth at any cost.

Boy: Where should I go to study the function of the human brain?
Girl: Just use your head.

Why was the old house crying?
It had windowpanes.

SIGN ON AN EYE DOCTOR'S OFFICE: If you don't see what you're looking for, you've certainly come to the right place.

Why do female deer never visit an optometrist?
Hind sight is 20/20.

Doctor: Do you really feel okay?
Grandfather: Yes. I'm old enough to know better.

SIGN IN A DERMATOLOGIST'S OFFICE: Give me some skin, dude!

LOONY EXIT LINES:

FOR LEO TOLSTOY: Rest in War and Peace.

FOR DOROTHY OF OZ: Gone with the Wind.

FOR HUMPTY DUMPTY: Rest in Pieces.

FOR BAMBI: Deerly Beloved.

FOR A BASEBALL PLAYER: Home at Last.

FOR A LAWYER: Case Closed Forever.

FOR A DETECTIVE: Arrest in Peace.

What do you call a dentist who works on a boat?
Offshore drilling.

A sick man drove himself to a hospital emergency room. "My gosh," said an intern to the man. "You're in a terrible state." The ill man gasped, "New Jersey isn't that bad."

Why did the window shade go to the psychologist?
It was up tight.

What did the arm bone say to the funny bone?
You're quite humerus.

Why are there always openings at a dentist's office?
They're always looking to fill holes.

Did you hear about the dentist who treated a ghost?
They had a brush with the supernatural.

Father: How did you make out at the pie-eating contest?
Boy: Not so good. My friend came in first and I came in sickened.

Why did the pirate take his trunk to the doctor?
It had a chest cold.

Patient: Help me, doctor. I think I'm invisible!
Doctor: Who said that?

Bill: I know an inexpensive surgeon.
Will: Does he do cut-rate operations?
Bill: No. He does cut-right operations.

NOTICE: A depressed dentist is a guy who always looks down in the mouth.

Why did the eagle go to the doctor?
He had a soar throat.

Doctor: Your cough sounds better today.
Boy: It should be. I practiced all night.

What do you call a national epidemic?
Germination.

◄ ◄ ◄ ◄ ◄ ◄ ◄ ◄ ◄ ◄ ◄ ◄ ◄ ◄ ◄ ◄

Why did Humpty Dumpty go to the hospital after his fall?
He was shell-shocked.

Hiker: My doctor keeps telling me to get plenty of fresh air, but he never tells me where to find it.

Tim: I think you have bucket fever.
Jim: Why do you think that?
Tim: You look kind of pail.

▶ ▶ ▶ ▶ ▶ ▶ ▶ ▶ ▶ ▶ ▶ ▶ ▶ ▶ ▶ ▶ ▶

Why do bridges make good doctors?
They help you get over your illness.

Lady: Doctor, my son used to love to go jogging. Now he thinks he's a car and won't run.
Doctor: It sounds like he has a gas problem.

CHAPTER 2

SPORTS SNICKERS

What do you call an invisible golf course?
The missing links.

What do you call a photograph of a baseball thrower hanging on the wall?
A pitcher framed.

Where do baseball batting champions march?
In a hit parade.

SIGN ON A WEIGHT ROOM: The weak ends here.

Who is the laziest person in sports?
The coach potato.

Penny: How many slopes did they have at the ski resort you went to?
Jenny: Three. There was a beginners' slope, an intermediate slope, and lastly, the final slope you'll ever ski.

Rick: *Do you ever take an illegal golf shortcut?*
Nick: *No. I always play the fairway.*

What kind of cookies do baseball players eat in Maryland?
Baltimore Oreos.

Nell: I'm a White Sox fan.
Dell: I'm a Red Sox fan.
Mel: I'm a fan of going barefoot.

What does a prizefighter wear on a hot day?
Boxer shorts.

What does a golfer who can't get a date use to hit his ball?
A lonely hearts club.

NOTICE: A caddy who stands behind a golfer and tells him how to hit the ball is a backseat driver.

What toy did the quarterback ask Santa to bring him?
A set of blocks.

KOOKY QUESTION:
Does a baseball player eat on home plates?

Zack: I'm not much of an athlete.
Mack: What do you mean?
Zack: I got tennis elbow playing golf.

SIGN ON A GOLF COURSE: Children's playground ahead. Drive carefully.

What do you get if you cross a busy highway with a skateboard?
A trip to the hospital.

Golfer: Have you noticed any improvement since last year?
Caddy: Yes. You bought a new set of clubs.

Which country makes the best rods and reels?
Poland.

Why did the cherry pull its car off the racetrack?
It was time for a pit stop.

What did the boxer say to the passing tornado?
Can I go around with you?

Wife: Why do you have to play golf every Saturday?
Husband: My doctor told me to take in more greens.

When is the best time to play golf?
At fore o'clock.

ATTENTION: If someone says, "I love tennis," do they have zero interest in sports?

▶ ▶ ▶ ▶ ▶ ▶ ▶ ▶ ▶

What do poker players like to get in December?
Christmas cards.

◀ ◀ ◀ ◀ ◀ ◀ ◀ ◀ ◀ ◀

What does a winning NASCAR driver have?
Wheels of fortune.

▶ ▶ ▶ ▶ ▶ ▶ ▶ ▶ ▶

Why did the egg quit the baseball team?
It couldn't crack the starting lineup.

◀ ◀ ◀ ◀ ◀ ◀ ◀ ◀ ◀ ◀ ◀ ◀ ◀ ◀ ◀ ◀ ◀

Why did the baseball player stay inside?
He was afraid of getting out.

▶ ▶ ▶ ▶ ▶ ▶ ▶ ▶ ▶ ▶ ▶ ▶ ▶ ▶ ▶ ▶ ▶ ▶ ▶ ▶

Why did the football coach ask for 25 cents?
He wanted a quarterback.

◀ ◀ ◀ ◀ ◀ ◀ ◀ ◀ ◀ ◀ ◀ ◀ ◀ ◀ ◀ ◀ ◀ ◀

Why did the detective take the baseball players to the police station?
To put them in his lineup.

▶ ▶ ▶ ▶ ▶ ▶ ▶ ▶ ▶ ▶ ▶ ▶ ▶ ▶ ▶ ▶ ▶ ▶ ▶

Why did the golfer cut part of his sock?
He wanted a hole in one.

◀ ◀ ◀ ◀ ◀ ◀ ◀ ◀ ◀ ◀ ◀ ◀ ◀ ◀ ◀ ◀ ◀ ◀

Band Student: **Our school orchestra played Beethoven last night.**
School Athlete: **Who won?**

What did the salt cheerleaders do?
They held a pepper rally.

▶ ▶ ▶ ▶ ▶ ▶ ▶ ▶ ▶ ▶ ▶ ▶ ▶ ▶ ▶ ▶ ▶ ▶ ▶ ▶

Why did the golfer get a ticket?
He was driving without a license.

◀ ◀ ◀ ◀ ◀ ◀ ◀ ◀ ◀ ◀ ◀ ◀ ◀ ◀ ◀ ◀ ◀ ◀ ◀ ◀

How do pool players play poker?
They use cue cards.

▶ ▶ ▶ ▶ ▶ ▶ ▶ ▶ ▶ ▶ ▶ ▶ ▶ ▶ ▶ ▶ ▶ ▶ ▶ ▶

What kind of boat did Babe Ruth own?
A dugout canoe.

◀ ◀ ◀ ◀ ◀ ◀ ◀ ◀ ◀ ◀ ◀

What do you call a quick sketch of
a New York baseball player?
A Yankee doodle.

▶ ▶ ▶ ▶ ▶ ▶ ▶ ▶ ▶ ▶ ▶ ▶

**Where did the baseball
player's union stage a rally?**
In the strike zone.

◀ ◀ ◀ ◀ ◀ ◀ ◀ ◀ ◀ ◀ ◀ ◀ ◀ ◀ ◀ ◀ ◀ ◀ ◀ ◀

Why was Mr. Locomotive so proud?
His son was a track star.

▶ ▶ ▶ ▶ ▶ ▶ ▶ ▶ ▶ ▶ ▶ ▶ ▶ ▶ ▶ ▶ ▶ ▶ ▶ ▶

Why do basketball players spend so much time at home?
Because they're not allowed to travel.

Why do scarecrows make great baseball players?
They're out standing in the field.

Why did the tennis player become a waiter?
He wanted to learn how to serve.

Why did the **NASCAR** driver buy four toupees?
His car had bald tires.

Fran: Did you hear about the hairdresser who became a bodybuilder?
Jan: No.
Fran: Now she's curling iron.

What do you get if you cross a good poker player with a golfer?
The Ace of Clubs.

Why are fishermen great singers? They know a tuna two.

What happened to the couch potato who tried to play quarterback?
He got sacked.

What did the driver say to the putter?
Let's go clubbing.

What do you call a high school golfer?
A student driver.

How do you light a fire under a lazy prizefighter?
Use a boxing match.

What do you call a funny bodybuilder?
A he-he-man.

What did one street racer say to the other?
This job is getting to be a real drag.

Show me a picnic meal outside of a baseball dugout and I'll show you players who step up to the plate.

Did you hear about the golfer with car troubles?
His engine kept puttering out.

Which sports channel do vipers watch?
E-Hiss-P-N.

What is coffee's favorite hockey team?
The Brewins.

What did one golf club say to the other?
Let's go for a drive.

What did the golfer carry for luck?
A fore-leaf clover.

Why did the football player buy a feather mattress?
He wanted to touchdown.

Joe: **I can tell you the score of any football game before the opening kickoff.**
Moe: **That's astonishing.**
Joe: **Not really. It's always zero to zero.**

What kind of tennis did they play on Noah's Ark?
Doubles.

Why does the boxer never silence his phone?
He likes the ring.

What do you get when you don't refrigerate an athlete?
A spoiled sport.

What is a couch potato's best golf stroke?
A chip shot.

How does a sprint runner take their coffee?
With a dash of cream.

What did the gymnast say when she broke up with her partner?
It's time we split.

Why did the football lineman go to a psychologist?
He was having problems with a mental block.

◀ ◀ ◀ ◀ ◀ ◀ ◀ ◀ ◀ ◀ ◀ ◀ ◀ ◀ ◀ ◀ ◀ ◀ ◀ ◀

When do boxers wear gloves?
When it's cold outside.

Dan: Did you hear about the football player who got a role in *A Midsummer Night's Dream*?
Stan: No, who did he play?
Dan: Puck.

Who invented the game of golf?
Our forefathers.

▶ ▶ ▶ ▶ ▶ ▶ ▶ ▶ ▶ ▶ ▶ ▶ ▶ ▶ ▶ ▶ ▶ ▶ ▶ ▶

What did the baseball manager say to his new infielder?
If at first you don't succeed, we'll try you at second or third base.

Beverly: Did you hear about the photographer who became a hockey player?
Waverly: Why did he do that?
Beverly: He wanted to trade his snapshots for slapshots.

What casts spells and plays croquet?
A wicket witch.

What did the baseball pitcher put on the floors of his house?
Throw rugs.

ATTENTION: Basketball players and earring photographers both shoot hoops.

Why did the mailman become a NASCAR driver?
He wanted to be in the post position.

Why didn't the Olympic diver run for political office?
He had no platform.

Mickey: My wife says she'll leave me if I don't give up golf.
Ricky: What are you going to do?
Mickey: I'm going to miss her a lot.

What do you get when surfers riot?
A beach brawl.

Where do small onions play baseball?
In the Little Leeks.

What does a librarian play golf with?
A book club.

Why did the salesman play baseball?
He wanted to work on his pitch.

What do you get when you cross a golfer and a NASCAR driver?
Someone who likes driving in circles all day long.

Where did the judge play on the court softball team?
Nowhere. The judge was on the bench.

ATTENTION: Is a bad golfer a bogeyman?

Why did the giant air conditioner go to a baseball game?
He was the world's biggest fan.

Golfer: I cut ten strokes off my golf game today.
Caddy: How did you do that?
Golfer: I didn't play the last hole.

Snow White: I heard you did well at the golf course.
Prince: How do you know?
Snow White: A little birdie told me.

ATTENTION: Pro boxers make money fist over fist.

Why are ghosts good at football?
They can go right through the other team's defense.

MOST TEAM SPIRIT

Why did the boxer wear a tutu and ballet shoes?
He wanted to dance around the ring.

Why did the boxer work at the training gym?
He wanted on-the-jab training.

Golfer: I've never played so badly.
Caddy: You mean you've played before?

Who do you get if you cross a
great centerfielder
with a cornfield?
Willie Maize.

Why did the cornerback
cover himself in glue?
His coach told him to
stick to the wide receiver.

How do you catch a Miami Dolphin?
Use tackle.

What does an Miami basketball fan do in the winter?
They turn on the Heat.

Soccer player: **What should I do if someone
kicks the ball high in the air?**
Coach: **Just use your head.**

Why is Cinderella so good at soccer?
All she wants to do is go to the ball.

What do you get if you cross a firefly with a famous Yankee hitter?
Glow DiMaggio.

Who is the meanest home-run hitter in history?
Babe Ruthless.

What is Captain Hook's favorite baseball team?
The Pittsburgh Pirates.

Which Hall of Fame baseball player became a shoe repairman?
Ty Cobbler.

What do you call a pair of pants running laps?
Joggers.

Why did the ice skater go to the desert?
She wanted to perfect her camel spin.

Why did the quarterback go to theatre school?
He wanted to learn all the plays.

KOOKY QUESTION: Do professional boxers have to punch a time clock when they work out?

Reporter: **What's it like to ride in the Tour de France year after year after year?**

Lance: **It's a vicious cycle.**

Coach: Yesterday the snail athletes held their 100-yard dash.

Reporter: Who won?

Coach: I don't know. We're still waiting for someone to finish.

Which football player is the least trustworthy?
The quarterback sneak.

What sport do athletic rodents play?
Mice hockey.

What do you find on a NASCAR zebra?
Racing stripes.

Bowler #1: When are you going to knock down those remaining pins?

Bowler #2: When I have some spare time.

What has a cow at shortstop, a sheep in centerfield, and a pig on the pitcher's mound?
A farm team.

What do you call four disorganized people playing tennis?
Mixed-up doubles.

What do you get if you teach martial arts to a goat?
The karate kid.

Why did the vampire become a NASCAR driver?
He always wanted to be a Drac racer.

Why did the football player wear a blank jersey?
He had an unlisted number.

What do you get when you cross a track hurdler with iguanas?
Leapin' lizards.

What should you do if you don't like a kickoff?
Just return it.

◄ ◄

How do you get a full backfield?
Feed them a big meal before the game.

Who delivers football fan mail?
The goal postman.

What do you call a blizzard in the middle of a football game?
A big halftime snow.

Why did the referee get a new phone?
Because he kept missing calls.

Defensive lineman: Hey, quarterback, will you run a play already?
Quarterback: Don't rush me.

What Hall of Fame linebacker
has webbed feet?
Duck Butkus.

Which pro football team is
named after a small bottle
of pop?
The Mini-soda Vikings.

▶ ▶ ▶ ▶ ▶ ▶ ▶ ▶ ▶ ▶ ▶ ▶ ▶ ▶
What's the biggest difference
between pro wrestling and pro
football?

In wrestling there are no holding penalties.
◀ ◀ ◀ ◀ ◀ ◀ ◀ ◀ ◀ ◀ ◀ ◀ ◀ ◀ ◀ ◀ ◀ ◀ ◀
Why do you call a duck that plays football?
A quarterquack.

What has wings and plays defensive line?
A flying tackle.

Why did the fullback wear swimming trunks?
The coach told him to run some dive plays.

What does a football team use on a rainy day?
An umbrella defense.

What has soft feathers and weighs three hundred pounds?
A down lineman.

What is the cleanest play in football?
A sweep play.

How do offensive linemen celebrate a victory?
They throw a block party.

Which football player tells the best sports stories?
The tale-back.

What made Santa happy while golfing?
He made a ho-ho-hole in one.

Why was the baseball player's mom so happy?
Because her son reached home safely.

Mr. Cereal: **What do you want to do today?**
Mr. Milk: **Let's bowl together.**

Why do vultures make great basketball players?
They always sink one in at the buzzard.

Why are kangaroos bad at
basketball?
They get in trouble
for carrying.

SLAM DUNK!

Which fish is the best basketball
player in the ocean?
Mackerel Jordan.

ATTENTION: Plumbers who play
golf know how to sink putts.

Fisherman: Not only am I a great caster, I'm also a good
basketball player.
Reporter: Oh, really?
Fisherman: Absolutely. I have a terrific hook shot.

What did the angry umpire say to the
bald baseball coach?
You're outta' hair!

Basketball player: You're giving me a speeding ticket?
Cop: Just think of it as a traveling violation.

Ryan: What do you think of Ivy League football?
Brian: It's vine with me.

NOTICE:

The Navy football team was penalized for trying to sneak a sub into the game.

Air Force football players are New York Jet supporters.

West Point football players always pay attention to formations.

What's a zombie's favorite position in soccer?
Ghoul keeper.

What do you call a pig who plays basketball?
A ball hog.

What do you get if you cross a running back with a sledgehammer?
A fullback who hits the line hard and breaks through a wall of tacklers.

Why did the football leave the stadium?
The punter kicked it out.

How did the quarterback celebrate Father's Day?
He threw a pop pass.

What do you get if you cross a pro wrestler with a defensive end?
A lineman who really throws the quarterback for a loss.

Why did the football player take up acting?
He wanted a part in a long-running play.

What kind of shirts do golfers wear?
Tee shirts.

NOTICE: A professional hockey goalie has a net income.

DAFFY DEFINITION:
Wrestling Mat: A pin cushion.

Why is a hockey goalie like the Lone Ranger?
They're both masked men.

What's the hottest part of a game of tennis?
The end of the match.

What is a bug's favorite sport?
Cricket.

Where did King Henry the VIII play tennis?
On his royal court.

What is Smokey the Bear's favorite ice hockey team?
The New York Forest Rangers.

....

What is a merman's favorite shirt?
A water polo.

....

Why did the patient with amnesia take up distance running?
He hoped it would jog his memory.

....

What do you get if you cross a tennis player and a comedian?
A court jester.

....

MESSAGE ON A BASEBALL PLAYER'S PHONE:
Sorry, I'm out.

....

What do you call a thief playing called-shot pool?
A picked pocket.

....

DAFFY DEFINITION:
NASCAR pit crew: people who tire quickly.

What do you call a baseball player relaxing in his backyard?
He's out at home.

....

Farmer Hitter: I just hit the ball into the chicken coop. That's a home run!
Farmer Fielder: No way! The chicken coop is fowl territory.

....

What do you call an angry person who competes in a marathon?
A very cross country runner.

YOU TELL 'EM SPORT

You tell 'em football center... and be snappy!

You tell 'em quarterback... don't pass up the chance.

You tell 'em heavyweight champ...you know the punch line.

You tell 'em hockey player... they'll love your slapstick humor.

You tell 'em soccer player... we'll all get a kick out of the story.

You tell 'em golfer...and drive home your point.

You tell 'em tennis star...and serve up a great story.

You tell 'em tight end... they'll catch on.

You tell 'em sprinter...you're a fast talker.

You tell 'em pitcher...they'll never believe the curve ball!

You tell 'em jogger...but don't run off at the mouth.

You tell 'em NASCAR driver...and don't race through the story.

What did the baseball pitcher say to the blackjack dealer?
Don't you dare hit me.

What do you get if you cross a prizefighter with a fast baseball pitcher?
A boxer who is hard to hit.

What kind of defense did the vampire basketball team use?
A twilight zone.

Where do golfers go to improve their game?
Drivers ed.

Where do pigs play baseball?
At the ballpork.

▶ ▶

What does an owl cheerleader shout?
Who-ray for our team!

◀ ◀

What do you get if you cross a library with a golfer?
Book clubs.

▶ ▶

What did the boxer say to the ref when he got
knocked down?
You can count on me.

◀ ◀

What kind of fans follow the New York Jets?
Just plane folks.

▶ ▶

What did the weightlifter say after bench-pressing
a three-hundred-pound barbell?
Phew! That's a load off of my chest.

◀ ◀

What do you call a male deer on ice skates?
Cold harted.

▶ ▶

**What do you get if you cross a speedy skier with
something that removes pencil marks?**
A downhill eraser.

◀ ◀

What did the ball say to the golf coach?
Putt me in, coach.

Why did the man wear swim trunks to play billiards?
He heard they were there for the pool.

▶ ▶

What do you get when you cross a baseball pitcher with a music box?
A pitcher who needs a windup.

◀ ◀

Which baseball player never goes to many games?
The left home fielder.

▶ ▶

Why didn't the screwdriver make the baseball team?
He could only pitch screwballs.

◀ ◀

Ben: Do old baseball players like rock 'n' roll?
Ken: No, they like swing music.

▶ ▶

Why are union leaders like baseball umpires?
They both have the power to call strikes.

◀ ◀

What did the batting coach say to the player named Swede Chariot when the pitcher started throwing him knee high fastballs?
Swing low, Swede Chariot!

▶ ▶ ▶ ▶ ▶ ▶ ▶ ▶ ▶

What do you get if you cross a baseball hurler with a certified letter?
A pitcher with a special delivery.

Why did the fast pitcher throw a slow ball?
It was a nice change of pace.

Why should you never buy tickets for an umpire?
He always misses plays.

◀ ◀ ◀ ◀ ◀ ◀ ◀ ◀ ◀ ◀ ◀ ◀ ◀ ◀ ◀ ◀ ◀ ◀ ◀

What do you call a zombie in a baseball diamond?
A dugout.

What do you get if you cross an infielder with a cello player?
An athlete who plays base fiddle.

DAFFY DEFINITION:
Professional skateboarder: Someone on the daily grind.

▶ ▶ ▶ ▶ ▶ ▶ ▶ ▶ ▶ ▶ ▶ ▶ ▶ ▶ ▶ ▶ ▶ ▶ ▶

How are baseball teams like pancakes?
They both need a good batter.

What has four wheels and is in the baseball Hall of Fame?
Connie Mack Truck.

Why do telemarketers make good referees?
They're great at making calls.

Mom: All Junior does is race around the house all day long.
Dad: He just wants to score a home run.

What has 18 legs and catches flies?
A baseball team.

What does a baseball team do if their field floods?
They paddle to safety in a dugout canoe.

What did the baseball umpire say after a long road trip?
Ah, there's no place like home.

What do you get if you cross an anchor with a baseball pitch?
A sinker ball.

What do you get if you cross a lawnmower with a baseball pitch?
A cut fastball.

What do you get if you cross a hockey rink with a baseball pitch?
A slider.

Pitcher: Why are you wearing an oven mitt?
Infielder: I may have to catch a sizzling line drive.

How are fences like baseball players?
They both run around the field.

Mack: Did you hear about the silk worms who ran a race?
Jack: No, who won?
Mack: It was a tie.

ATTENTION:
Athletic beavers play stickball.

ATTENTION: Wooden bats have tree strikes in them.

What do you get if you cross an outfielder with a frog?
A player who is great at catching flies.

SIGN IN AN OUTFIELDER'S SEAFOOD RESTAURANT:
Come in for our catch-of-the-day special.

Billy: Uh-oh! It's a run home.
Willie: Don't you mean a home run?
Billy: Nope! I just hit the ball through the neighbor's window.

Where do baseball officials hold their yearly convention?
At the Umpire State Building.

▶ ▶

Why did the sheep umpire get fired?
It made too many baad calls.

◀ ◀ ◀ ◀ ◀ ◀ ◀ ◀ ◀ ◀ ◀ ◀ ◀

What do you get if you cross a baseball official with a vacuum?
An umpire who keeps home plate really, really clean.

▶ ▶ ▶ ▶ ▶ ▶ ▶ ▶ ▶ ▶ ▶ ▶

NOTICE: Hall of Fame batter Ty Cobb couldn't sing a note, but he had a lot of records.

◀ ◀ ◀ ◀ ◀ ◀ ◀ ◀ ◀ ◀ ◀

Why do vipers make bad baseball players?
They always strike out.

Why did the soccer player take ballet?
He wanted to work on his footwork.

ATTENTION: Hockey players with hot tempers are taught to rink before they speak.

KOOKY QUESTIONS AND ANSWERS:

What do you find at the end of an athlete's leg? Athletes foot!

What do you see when you walk out on one Broadway show and go to another one? A double play!

What do you call a pool ball with the number three on it? Oddball!

DO THEY COME IN SIZE 6½?

What does a racehorse wear when he's not wearing slippers? Horseshoes!

What do you do when you pet a baby duck? Touchdown!

Why was the basketball player a bad fisherman? He caught nothing but net.

What part of the basketball court smells the most? The foul line.

What do you call a sports fan who tries to excite a tired crowd? The cheerman of the bored.

Coach: How do you feel about competing in the high jump event?

Athlete: There were a lot of hurdles on my way getting here.

Why are chickens bad at baseball?
They keep getting fowls.

Why did the jogger get arrested?
He ran with a bad crowd.

Hockey player: I really need a job. Can't you give me some ice time?
Hockey coach: Sorry. We're in the middle of a hiring freeze.

What do you get if you cross a NASCAR racer with a thunderstorm?
Driving rain.

What do you get if you cross a NASCAR racer with a stove?
A driving range.

Why are NASCAR drivers always lost?
Because they never make a right turn.

Gymnast: Who gets the last slice of pizza?
Acrobat: I'll flip you for it.

Athlete: I want to set a world record in the pole vault.
Coach: Gee, you have high hopes.

Boy #1: I'd like to meet that professional bowler.
Boy #2: Well, walk over there and strike up a conversation.

DAFFY DEFINITIONS:
Bowling team: Pin pals.
Bowler: A roll player.

What kind of cats like to go bowling?
Alley cats.

What is a baker's favorite football play?
A roll-out pass.

Track star: I don't like to high jump before noon.
Coach: Why not?
Track star: I find it hard to get up in the morning.

What do you get if you cross a ping pong set with a canoe?
A paddle boat.

What did the angry race horse say to the jockey?
Get off of my back already!

Mountains play valleyball. Rivers run. What do gardens do?
Mostly they just veg out.

Show me a football kicker who sharpens pencils at both ends and I'll show you a guy who makes extra points.

Sally: Did you see the Olympic archers practicing?
Ally: Yes! Their outfits were quite fletching.

Why did the baseball closer take an electric blanket into the bullpen?
He needed it in case he had to warm up fast.

What do you get if you cross an octopus with a tailback?
A runner who gives a lot of stiff arms.

Why did the racehorse go for counseling?
He was saddled with a lot of personal problems.

Did you hear about the zombie runner?
They finished in dead last.

What did the hockey coach say to the player who was caught breaking team rules?
Watch your step! You're skating on thin ice.

What do you get if you cross an accountant with an ice rink?
A figure skater.

Zeke: Why is your racing car in the shape of a banana?
Deak: I like to peel out.

Golfer #1: Your ball landed in a mud puddle.
Golfer #2: That's a dirty lie.

What position does the sun play in football?
The star quarterback.

Show me a bike racer speeding down a road and I'll show you a street pedaler.

Why did the golf club rush to the hospital?
It was having a stroke.

How did the tennis player get his girlfriend to marry him?
He courted her.

Why did the politician take up jogging over the summer?
Because he had to run for re-election in the fall.

Which member of the Rolling Stones rock band likes to run laps?
Mick Jogger.

What happens when young cows do lots of leg lifts?
They get great calf muscles.

ATTENTION: A husband and wife who jog together are running mates.

What do you get if you cross a NASCAR driver with a basketball player?
A player who knows how to drive down the lane.

ATTENTION: Basketball players who study law make good judges because they know how to run a court.

What do you get if you cross a basketball point guard with a gardener?
A give-and-grow play.

Coach: Have you found a permanent home yet?
Basketball player: No. I keep bouncing from one team to another.

Then there was the soccer star who tried out for the basketball team and got cut because he kept dribbling with his feet.

NOTICE: A nervous basketball player is very jumpy.

What do you get if you cross a basketball timer with a chicken?
A shot cluck!

ATTENTION: Lumberjacks who play basketball take lots of tree-point shots.

Why do basketball players make great photographers?
They always take great shots.

How are boxers like viral videos?
They both get a lot of hits.

What do you get if a fighter wears designer shoes in the ring?
A boxer with fancy footwork.

What do you get if you cross a baseball pitcher with a boxer?
A guy who throws the fight.

What do you get if you cross a boxer with an octopus?
I don't know, but it throws a lot of punches.

Manager: Was your party a success?
Boxer: It was a real knockout.

Jenny and Mia were professional boxers scheduled to fight each other. Before the first round, Jenny asked her manager what she had to do to win the bout. Her manager replied, "Sock it to Mia!"

▶ ▶ ▶ ▶ ▶ ▶ ▶ ▶ ▶ ▶ ▶ ▶ ▶ ▶ ▶ ▶ ▶

What's the most important thing for a boxing referee to know?
How to count to ten.

◀ ◀ ◀ ◀ ◀ ◀ ◀ ◀ ◀ ◀ ◀ ◀ ◀ ◀ ◀ ◀ ◀

What do you call a small nick on a boxer's forehead?
An upper cut.

▶ ▶ ▶ ▶ ▶ ▶ ▶ ▶ ▶ ▶ ▶ ▶ ▶ ▶ ▶ ▶ ▶

Why don't bicycles exercise?
They're two tired.

◀ ◀ ◀ ◀ ◀ ◀ ◀ ◀ ◀ ◀ ◀ ◀ ◀ ◀ ◀ ◀ ◀

Why don't trees exercise?
Working out saps their strength.

▶ ▶ ▶ ▶ ▶ ▶ ▶ ▶ ▶ ▶ ▶ ▶ ▶ ▶ ▶ ▶ ▶

Why don't mountains lift weights?
They're already rock hard.

◀ ◀ ◀ ◀ ◀ ◀ ◀ ◀ ◀ ◀ ◀ ◀ ◀ ◀ ◀ ◀ ◀

What's the best way to catch a fish?
Have someone pitch it to you.

▶ ▶ ▶ ▶ ▶ ▶ ▶ ▶ ▶ ▶ ▶ ▶ ▶ ▶ ▶ ▶ ▶

Why did the rabbit go to the pool?
To practice springboard diving.

◀ ◀ ◀ ◀ ◀ ◀ ◀ ◀ ◀ ◀ ◀ ◀ ◀ ◀ ◀ ◀ ◀

I knew a magician who played ice hockey and scored a lot of hat tricks.

Where did the clams go to work out?
Mussel beach.

What did the angry coach say to the basketball player?
When I give an order, you jump.

Why didn't the power plant play sports?
It didn't have enough energy.

Why is a soldier absent without leave like a baseball player who takes a huge lead?
Because they'll both be in trouble if they don't get back to base.

Why is Swiss cheese like a golf course?
They both have a lot of holes.

When is a horse race not won by a horse?
When it's won by a nose.

What sport only allows its athletes to take one jump at a time?
Sky diving.

What do you get if you cross fencing with water polo?
A swordfish's favorite sport.

Coach: *Would you like to try out for the fencing team?*
Athlete: *I'll take a stab at it.*

What do you get if you cross a gymnast with a miniature girl from a fairy tale?
Tumbelina.

Man #1: I compete in dogsled competitions.
Man #2: Oh! You're a race cur driver.

What do you get if you cross a martial arts expert with a lumberjack?
A person who karate chops wood.

Golfer #1: That was the best drive of my life! Let's celebrate right now.
Caddy: Okay. I'll arrange a tee party.

Why do pool players make bad pitchers?
They're known for throwing eight balls.

What do you call a surfing celebration?
A boarding party.

What is a carpenter's favorite track and field event?
The hammer throw.

SILLY SPORTS TITLE REVIEWS

Weightlifting Made Easy - a strong ending.

How to Size Up a Putting Green - really drives its point home.

How to Run Fast - a quick read.

Improve Your Biceps - a good book to curl up with.

Train for a Marathon - terrific from start to finish.

The Game of Golf - a book with a driving plot.

How to Intercept Passes - a good pick.

Why did the tennis fan go to an eye doctor?
Because every time he watched a match he saw doubles.

Gymnast: Do you mind if I jump over the vaulting horse?
Coach: No. Hop to it.

Why wasn't the lace put in the pair of football spikes?
It was third-string.

Farm Fielder: Hey, no fair! You hit the ball into the pigpen and a hog swallowed it.
Farm Batter: Tough luck. It's an inside-the-pork homerun!

SILLY SPORTS NAMES

Ron Fast the track star

Mike D. Tackle the football star

Teal A. Base the baseball star

Carl D. Play the umpire

Hud L. Upp the football star

Harry A. Long the marathon runner

Forest Down the football wide receiver

S.P. Lashe the diving star

NOTICE: SpongeBob tried out for football, but only made the scrub team.

What did the nervous pitcher say to the homerun hitter?
How'd you like to take a walk?

Show me a chicken roosting in a judge's chambers and I'll show you a backcourt fowl.

What do you get if you cross a baseball official with a judo expert?
An umpire who throws players out of the game.

Why are soccer players so successful?
Because they spend their lives moving toward goals.

Why did the baseball batter go into the music business?
He wanted to produce some big hits.

What does Scrooge wear on his feet to play ice hockey?
Cheap skates.

Why is a track team like a sleigh?
They both need good runners.

What is the wrong way to buy a tennis racket?
With no strings attached.

Who barks signals to the pitcher from behind the plate?
The dog catcher.

Show me a baseball hitter who stores his gear in a church steeple and I'll show you a person with bats in his belfry.

Jogger #1: Do you have a fever?
Jogger #2: No. It's only a runny nose.

What do you call the place pigs skateboard?
A skate pork.

Why is a middle infielder like a farm hand?
They're both good in the field.

Why is a wrestler like a bowler?
They both want to score a lot of pins.

Why did the caterpillar go out for the swim team?
He wanted to learn the butterfly stroke.

What did the goldfish do for fun?
It went bowling.

Why don't tennis newlyweds care if they're poor?
Because in tennis, when you have nothing, it's really love.

ATTENTION: When gophers play against moles in football, the contest is decided by which team has a better ground game.

Knock! Knock!
Who's there?
Nas.
Nas who?
NASCAR driver!

Show me a baseball batter on the top level of a cruise ship and I'll show you a player standing on deck.

NUTTY TRACK NAMES:

Hy Hurdles

Maury Thon

Paul Vaulter

Miles Torun

Sign on a NASCAR deli: **We serve wheel good food.**

Then there was the marathon runner who ran for 2 hours but only moved two feet.

What does a minister wear to play street hockey?
Holy roller blades.

Who cheers for Smokey and Yogi when they play baseball?
The root bear.

Why should you never race against a barber?
They know all the best shortcuts.

What do you get if you cross an outfielder with a track sprinter?
A baseball player who makes a lot of running catches.

What do you call a new ice hockey player?
A rink amateur.

Why don't drivers eat before the big race?
In case they get indy-gestion.

Then there was the football quarterback who became an author and wrote a football play.

And then there was the baseball batter who became a play producer and had a hit show on Broadway.

Finally there was the heavyweight fighter who became a comedy writer and penned some classic punch lines.

What's the difference between bowling and baseball?
In bowling, three strikes are good.

Which Hall of Fame baseball catcher loves to eat sandwiches?
Hoagie Berra.

What did the wrestler say when someone called his phone during a match?
Can I put you on hold?

What do you call a football player who hurries through a gorge?
A pass rusher.

What do you get if you cross an athlete with a lucky charm?
A sporting chance.

What do you get when you cross a ghost with a basketball?
Hoopernatural activity.

What kind of lotion do acrobats use?
Cirque d'Olay.

What do you get if you cross a minister and a sportscaster?
A pray-by-play announcer.

Why did the wrestler go to college?
He wanted to get a fraternity pin.

What does a prizefighter wear on his finger?
A boxing ring.

What do you get when a boxer meets a giant orange in the ring?
Fruit punch.

What do you need when twins play golf?
Tee for two.

Which football player is very itchy?
The flea safety.

Show me a hockey goalie who puts glue in his glove and I'll show you a player who makes a lot of stick saves.

What's a wrestling chef's signature move?
A soufflex.

Why did the cheerleader go to the dentist?
She needed a root-root-root canal.

Why is it good to be punctual if you're a football running back?
Because then you never have to rush to score a touchdown.

How can you tell if two elephants are prizefighters? They both have boxing trunks.

▶ ▶ ▶ ▶ ▶ ▶ ▶

What kind of retro dance did the boxer go to?
He went to a sock hop.

▶ ▶

KOOKY QUESTION: Do astronomers who are sports fans root for all-star teams?

▶ ▶

Jack: Is it easy to play offensive center?
Zack: Sure. The position is a snap.

▶ ▶

What did one baseball player say to the other while they were fishing?
Let's play a game of catch.

▶ ▶

What happened when SpongeBob pitched for his baseball team?
He got sent to the showers.

▶ ▶

How does a quarterback unlock his car?
He uses a pass key.

ATTENTION: Bus drivers who are sports fans love Greyhound racing.

◄ ◄

What do you call coffee brewed at a baseball stadium?
Ball perk.

◄ ◄!

Does a quarterback stop to pay tolls?
No. He uses his E-Z Pass.

◄ ◄

What do you call a monkey that wins the Super Bowl?
A chimpion.

◄ ◄ ◄ ◄ ◄ ◄ ◄ ◄ ◄

SIGN ON A GOLFER'S DELI:
Sink your teeth into our
new club sandwich.

◄ ◄ ◄ ◄ ◄ ◄ ◄ ◄ ◄

Spy guy: How do you destroy a baseball field?

James Bond: You can't destroy a baseball field. Diamonds are forever.

◄ ◄

NOTICE: People needed to pack crates. No experience necessary. We give free boxing lessons.

◄ ◄

Who is responsible for keeping the baseball stadium neat and tidy?
The clean-up hitter.

What did the golfer say to his rolling ball?
Stay putt.

What do you get if you cross sports enthusiasts with a driver and a nine iron?
Fan clubs.

Then there was the softball star named Kitty who pitched a purrfect game.

ATTENTION: Tornadoes make great football players because they always touchdown.

What do you get if you cross a hunting dog with a basketball player?
A pointer guard.

Why did the baseball batter break up with the softball pitcher?
They just didn't hit it off.

What did one football official say to the other after a big pile-up over a fumble?
Quick! Let's get to the bottom of this!

Did you hear the one about the bad pole-vaulter?
It never goes over very well.

What do you get if you cross a football player with an armadillo?
A player with built-in padding.

Why is football like baseball?
Both games usually have a lot of hits.

NOTICE: When a cyclist is deep in thought, you can hear the wheels turning.

What do you call tag-team wrestlers who are best friends?
Pin pals.

What do you get if you cross a catcher with an offensive tackle?
A baseball player who knows how to block the plate.

What do you get if you cross a baseball with a clumsy rabbit?
Ground balls that take a lot of bad hops.

What do you get if you cross a billiards player with a football blocker?
A pooling guard.

What kind of steaks do golfers like best?
Tee-bone steaks.

What did the boxer give Santa Claus?
Christmas punch.

Then there was the psychic baseball pitcher who didn't need to get signals from his catcher. He just read his mind.

Did you hear about the sports store selling baseballs?
They made quite the sales pitch.

What is the Jolly Green Jockey's favorite vegetable?
Horseradish.

Then there was the quarterback who called all running plays because he saw a sign outside the stadium that read, "This is a no passing zone."

Did you hear about the football captain who didn't believe he lost the coin toss and asked to see it on instant replay?

Our middle linebacker is so tough that as a child he didn't have a teddy bear. He slept with a live grizzly.

What do you get when you cross a football team and a gourmet cook?

The Kansas City Chefs.

Which football players are the most well-behaved?
Punters; they always put their best foot forward.

Man: Pro football tickets in New York cost too much.
Fan: It's a small price to pay for a Giant victory.

Coach: How fast can you run?
Player: That depends.
Coach: On what?
Player: Who's chasing me.

Joe: Did you hear about the quarterback who got everything backwards?

Moe: No. Tell me.

Joe: Every time he stepped up to the line to call signals, he yelled: "Tuh! Tuh! Tuh!"

Football Coach: Hit 'em high! Hit 'em low!
Player: Well, make up your mind already.

Lou: **Did you hear about the lineman's kid?**
Stew: **No, what's he like?**
Lou: **He's a chip off the old blocker.**

Hockey Player: Last year I broke my nose in five places.
Sports Reporter: Really?
Hockey Player: Yup. Pittsburgh, Buffalo, Montreal, Toronto, and Philadelphia.

What do you call a football player who builds houses?
A carpunter.

Did you hear about the insect who was kicked off the football team?
He was a real fumble bee.

The New York Giants signed an offensive lineman who was so big he took a taxi home after the game. The next day the police made him carry it back to the stadium parking lot.

Rumor has it that the Grand Canyon was formed when Paul Bunyan took up golf.

Then there was the baseball umpire who was a fortune-teller and called plays before they happened.

Once there was a baseball manager who thought he needed a giant python to pull off a squeeze play.

Why do football players make good janitors?
They're always running sweep plays.

If golf is good exercise for your heart, why do older golfers have so many strokes?

Why do football players wear helmets on their heads?
They don't fit on their feet.

Then there was the bad pitcher who was sent to the showers so often he quit baseball and took up swimming.

Old quarterbacks don't die. They just pass away.

Then there was the pro fighter who quit boxing to join the circus because he wanted to be a ringmaster.

Then there was the college football coach who hired a drivers ed instructor to teach his offense how to drive the ball down the field.

Of course, you've heard about the wacky hockey goalie that wore a different Halloween mask every game.

What do you get if you cross a kangaroo and a quarterback?
A pocket passer.

Caddy: Are you a Democrat or a Republican?
Golfer: Neither. I'm a member of the Tee Party.

Which season do hockey players dislike?
They could do without a fall.

What do you get if you cross an outfielder with a born loser?
A guy who can't catch a break.

What did the barbell say to the bodybuilder?
Hey dude! How about a lift?

Why is a tennis court so noisy?
Because tennis players always raise a racket.

Why did the Green Giant have to leave the baseball game?
The pitcher beaned him.

NOTICE: Golf carts are good for long drives.

What do you get if you cross athletes and NASCAR vehicles?
Sports cars.

Did you hear about the silent bowling alley?
It was so quiet you could hear a pin drop.

....

What do bowlers and Thanksgiving guests have in common?
They both want a turkey.

....

Caddy: Sir, you just scored a hole-in-one on the 18th hole.
Golfer: Yippee!
Caddy: Calm down sir, we're only on the 9th hole.

....

Baseball reporter: Have you ever been trapped between bases when the infielders have the ball?
Player: Heck no! I wouldn't be caught dead in a rundown place like that.

....

Mother: Why aren't you having fun at the skate park?
Son: Because I'm skate bored.

....

How does a movie director start a rollerblade race?
He yells, "Roll 'em!"

....

Which bird is a famous skateboarder?
Tony Hawk.

Why did the hipster fall in the lake?
He tried to go ice skating before it was cool.

What do you get if you cross a baseball player and a surfer?
A person who knows how to catch waves.

What do you call an athlete who plays baseball, football, tennis, soccer, golf and basketball?
A jock of all trades.

Who rode waves in Medieval England?
Serf boarders.

Why are comedians not allowed to ice skate?
They make the ice crack up.

What hat wears rollerblades?
The roller derby.

DAFFY DEFINITION:
Skateboarding: Wheel entertainment.

What makes a golfer happy?
His glee club.

What do sport coaches and dentists have in common?
They both use drills.

▷ ▷

Why did the golfer hit Abe with a club?
He wanted to drive a Lincoln.

◁ ◁

Knock! Knock!
Who's there?
Golan.
Golan who?
Golan, I'll throw you a deep pass.

▷ ▷

Tim: **Do punters ever get cut from a football team?**
Jim: **No. They get kicked off the squad.**

◁ ◁

Football tackle: I heard you were dead.
Punter: No. I'm still alive and kicking.

▷ ▷

What did the catcher's mitt say to the baseball?
Catch you later!

CHAPTER 3

FAMILY FUN

What did the butcher say to her boyfriend?
I can't wait to meat your family.

▶ ▶ ▶ ▶ ▶ ▶ ▶ ▶ ▶ ▶ ▶ ▶ ▶ ▶ ▶ ▶ ▶ ▶

Millie: Is that Mrs. Margarine's husband?
Tillie: No. It's her butter-in-law.

Who was Alexander the Lesser?
He was Alexander the Great's not-so-famous cousin.

Mother: Why are you crying?
Boy: My teeth stepped on my tongue.

◀ ◀ ◀ ◀ ◀ ◀ ◀ ◀ ◀ ◀ ◀ ◀ ◀ ◀ ◀ ◀ ◀ ◀ ◀

Son: Dad, can you tell me what a solar eclipse is?
Father: No sun.

Father: The new baby looks just like me.
Aunt: That doesn't matter as long as he's healthy.

My sister bet I couldn't make a car out of spaghetti.
You should have seen her face when I drove pasta.

Son: Yuck! I made really sour lemonade.
Mother: Well you're old enough to know bitter.

What do you call a priest that becomes a lawyer?
A father in law.

What do you call it when your sister watches a sad movie?
A cry sis.

What did one cell say to his sister cell when she stepped on his toe?
Mitosis.

Husband: Why are you knitting three socks?
Wife: Our daughter said her new baby has grown a foot since we last saw him.

▶ ▶ ▶ ▶ ▶ ▶ ▶ ▶ ▶ ▶ ▶ ▶ ▶ ▶ ▶ ▶ ▶ ▶ ▶

Little Broom: When were you born, Dad?
Father: I was a baby broomer.

What did the bedroom say to the sloppy teenager?
Here's another fine mess you've gotten me into.

What do werewolves read to
their children at bedtime?
Furry tail stories.

Mother: **Don't swim on
a full stomach.**
Son: **Okay, Mom. I'll do
the backstroke.**

**What did the tidy mom tell
her sloppy kids?**
Quit messing around the house.

"Take me to the fifth floor please," said the young company president to the elevator operator. The operator smiled and nodded. Soon the elevator car jerked to a stop.
"Here you are, son," said the elevator operator.
"How dare you call me son!" snapped the snobby company president.
"Hey! I brought you up didn't I?" replied the operator.

NOTICE: Mr. & Mrs. Emory Board just filed for divorce.

Grandmother: How long does your father sleep on Sunday morning?
Little Girl: That depends.
Grandmother: On what?
Little Girl: The length of our pastor's sermon.

Husband: Last night I dreamed I fixed our leaky sink.
Wife: That was just another one of your pipe dreams.

Son: Hey, Mom! Look at the huge fish I caught.
Mom: Wowie! That's a real whopper. Did your father catch anything?
Son: Yes. I used what Dad caught as bait to hook this monster.

Jed: My dad has Abe Lincoln's old potato peeler.
Ned: That's nothing. My dad has Adam's apple.

What did Albert Einstein say when asked about his family reunion?
It's all relatives.

What did the Invisible Boy call his Invisible Mom and Dad?
His transparents.

Patient: Can you cure me, doctor?
Doctor: I'm afraid not. Your illness is hereditary.
Patient: In that case, send the bill to my parents.

What did the parents say when they decided to toilet train their infant?
It's potty time!

Uncle Moe asked his nephew Harold if his two-year-old brother Morty had started to talk yet. "Why should Morty talk?" Harold said. "He gets everything he wants by hollering."

A girl was mailing a bible to her grandmother. The postal clerk asked if her package contained anything breakable. The girl smiled and replied, "Only the Ten Commandments."

KOOKY QUESTION: If identical siblings are both interested in something, do they have twin piques?

Joey: When my grandpa sneezes, he always puts his hand over his mouth.
Zoey: To stop germs from spreading?
Joey: No, to catch his teeth.

What do you call two siblings who take your money?
Fine brothers.

My sister, my aunt, and my mother all have holes in their tights.
It runs in the family.

Son: Can I go out tonight?
Father: With so much homework?
Son: No, with my girlfriend.

Don: My parents got mad at me for talking about ducks.
Juan: What? Why?
Don: They told me not to use fowl language.

Cherry: There goes Grandpa Pie.
Plum: He's a crusty old guy.

Father: Stop misbehaving and I'll tell you the joke about the big Christmas present.
Boy: And if I don't stop misbehaving?
Father: Then you won't get it.

A father gives flowers to all of his family members. To his wife, he gives roses, to his daughter, he gives daisies, and to his son, he gives sunflowers.

When I was younger my parents made me walk the plank. We couldn't afford a dog.

Uncle Al: *I know I'm ugly. Last Christmas my parents gave me a turtleneck sweater that had no hole for my head.*

Lindy: My husband is such a couch potato during the football season.
Cindy: Does he root for the home team?

What did the mom fire say to the dad fire?
I'm so proud of arson.

Did you hear about the former straight-A student who got in trouble with his parents?
Looks like he was stung by a B.

Ken: My uncle is now with the FBI.
Len: I knew they'd catch up with him sooner or later.

Son: When I grow up, I want to drive a steamroller.
Father: Well in that case, son, I won't stand in your way.

Chester: I heard your sister married a second lieutenant.
Lester: Yeah. The first one got away.

Little Boy: Mom! I spilled a six-pack of soda all over the stovetop.
Mom: Oh great! Foam on the range.

What did Santa Claus get when he filed for a divorce?
An independent Claus.

Mother: All right, who put dirty fingerprints all over the newly painted wall? Was it Matthew or Marty?
Marty: It was Matthew, Mom. I saw him at the scene of the grime.

Dora: We named our son after English royalty.
Nora: Really? What do you call him?
Dora: The Prince of Wails.

Why did the daydreamer disobey his parents?
It kept him grounded.

My parents warned me about procrastination.
I told them, "Just you wait."

Why do doctors make good parents?
They have plenty of patients.

Anne: How many relatives were at your family picnic?
Jan: There were six uncles and about a million ants.

Boy: I did two good deeds today. I went to see Aunt Stacy.
Father: That's only one good deed.
Boy: No it's two. Aunt Stacy was happy when I went to see her. She was even happier when I finally left.

A small girl greeted a visiting relative at the door. It was her mother's sister. "I'm glad you came, Aunt Clara," said the girl. "Now dad will do the trick he talked about." Aunt Clara was confused. "What trick?" she asked her little niece. "Dad said if you came to visit, he'd climb the walls for sure."

Monster Dad: Where's my cloak? Where's my shovel? Where's my axe?
Monster Boy: I'm hungry, Mom.
Monster Girl: Help me frizz my hair, Mom.
Monster Mom: Calm down all of you and be patient. I only have four hands.

Teenage Girl: What a beautiful car. Let's go buy it.
Father: Right. Let's go right by it.

Aunt: Don't children brighten up a home?
Father: Absolutely! They never turn off any lights.

Jack: My uncle cleaned up on Wall Street.
Mack: Is he an investor?
Jack: No. A janitor.

Cabin Boy #1: My grandfather dug the Panama Canal.
Cabin Boy #2: Big deal. My uncle killed the Dead Sea.

Father: Do you want me to help you swing that baseball bat, son?
Boy: No Dad. It's time for me to strike out on my own.

Jill: My father makes sofas all day.
Bill: What does he do when he comes home?
Jill: He sleeps on his job.

What did Mr. and Mrs. Drum name their twin sons?
Tom-Tom.

What did the mom printer say to the daughter printer?
Don't speak to me in that tone of voice!

Kelly: I decided to cook a big surprise dinner for my family the other night.

Nelly: They must have been so surprised!

Kelly: They would have been, if the fire trucks hadn't given it away.

Mother: Billy! Stop reaching across the dinner table. Don't you have a tongue?
Billy: Yes, Mom, but my arms are longer.

"Donna, what happened to our pet canary?" a mother asked her daughter. "The cage is empty. The bird is gone." "Hmm," answered the little girl. "That's funny. It was there a minute ago when I vacuumed out its cage."

My parents won't say which of their six kids they love the best, but they told me I finished just out of the top five.

Ted: How old is your great-grandfather?
Jed: I'm not sure, but he must be pretty old. His social security number is one.

Tina: My son came to visit for summer vacation.
Deana: How nice! Did you meet him at the airport?
Tina: Oh, no. I've known him for years!

What do you call a fish's dad?
The cod father.

Mother: I told you to wash your hands. Look at those filthy wrists.
Boy: Ah, gee, Mom. A guy has to draw the line somewhere.

Mother: When it comes to cleaning his room, my teenage son likes to do nothing better.

Mother: Marty! Are you spitting in the goldfish bowl?
Marty: No Mom, but I'm getting closer with every try.

Did you hear about the dad who bought his son a fridge for Christmas?
He couldn't wait to see his son's face light up when he opened it.

The son of a very wealthy family was sent to a public school so he'd learn to get along with average people. "Now don't tell anyone we're rich son," said his father. "Act like we're very poor and everyone will like you." "Okay father," promised the rich youngster. The boy's first day in school he was asked to write a composition about his family to be read in front of the class. "We're poor," read the boy. "My dad is poor. My mom is poor. Our butler is poor. Our maids are poor. Our chauffeur is poor. The cook and the gardener are poor. I'm just a regular poor kid."

What did the big raindrop say to the little raindrop?
My plop is bigger than your plop.

Father: Why did your friend Tim get an A on his homework while you only got a C?
Boy: Tim has smarter parents.

◀ ◀

What did the calf say to the silo?
Is my fodder in there?

Phil: My uncle made a fortune in crooked dough.
Jill: Is he a counterfeiter?
Phil: No. A pretzel maker.

Boy: My name is Seven and a Quarter.
Girl: Where'd you get a silly name like that?
Boy: My parents picked it out of a hat.

What does a disappointed mother turkey tell her kids?
If your father were to see you now, he would be turning over in his gravy!

Mom: Billy! Why didn't you answer me?
Billy: I did. I shook my head.
Mom: Well did you expect me to hear it rattle all the way upstairs?

A boy handed his report card to his father. "Dad," said the boy. "Remember at the start of school you said if I got all 'A's on my report card you'd give me a fifty dollar bill?" The father smiled. "I remember son, and I'll keep my word." "Well Pop," said the boy. "I just saved you fifty bucks!"

Boy: I know a kid who eats out of garbage cans.
Mother: That's horrible. What kind of parents does he have?
Boy: They're goats.

Boy: My folks are sending me to summer camp.
Girl: Why? Do you need a vacation?
Boy: No. They do.

▶ ▶

Father: Before we hike to our campsite let's check our gear. Phones? Tablets? Laptops? Instant gourmet food?
Son: We have all of that, Dad.
Father: Good. Let's go. I'm looking forward to roughing it.

◀ ◀

Brother: I told Mom and Dad I wanted to be a comedian.
Sister: What did they say?
Brother: Nothing. All they did was laugh.

▶ ▶ ▶ ▶ ▶ ▶ ▶ ▶ ▶ ▶ ▶ ▶ ▶ ▶ ▶ ▶ ▶ ▶ ▶ ▶

Reporter: I understand you started to train for a career in the boxing ring as a child?
Boxer: True. My parents made me sit in the corner a lot.

◀ ◀ ◀ ◀ ◀ ◀ ◀ ◀ ◀ ◀

ATTENTION: My grandfather had the heart of a lion and a lifetime ban from the local zoo.

▶ ▶ ▶ ▶ ▶ ▶ ▶ ▶ ▶ ▶ ▶ ▶ ▶ ▶ ▶ ▶ ▶ ▶ ▶

Mother: Robert, share your new sled with your little brother.
Robert: I am, Mom. I use it going down the slope and he gets to use it going up it.

What kind of music should you listen to on Father's Day?
Pop music.

▶ ▶

Son: I only told one lie this month.
Father: When was that?
Son: Just now.

◀ ◀ ◀ ◀ ◀ ◀ ◀

Big Brother: Don't you think it's time we took our little brother to the zoo?
Sister: If they want him, let them come and get him.

▶ ▶

Mom: I sent you to the store and you brought home the wrong thing.
Daughter: What's wrong with the margarine I got?
Mom: Nothing, but you're old enough to know butter.

◀ ◀ ◀ ◀ ◀ ◀ ◀ ◀ ◀ ◀ ◀ ◀ ◀ ◀ ◀ ◀ ◀ ◀ ◀ ◀

Mother: Johnny, did you eat the entire package of cookies?
Johnny: I didn't touch one.
Mother: But there's only one left.
Johnny: That's the one I didn't touch.

Did you hear about the cable company that's going to have a baby?
They're expecting a bundle of joy.

Boy: Doctor, first my uncle thought he was a door key. Now he thinks he's a doorknob.
Doctor: It sounds like he's taken a turn for the worse.

Mel: My father is the greatest dad in the world.
Stella: How do you know that?
Mel: He's number one on all the pop charts.

Boy: My name is Paste.
Man: Is that your brother?
Boy: Yes. His name is Glue.
We stick together.

Boy: My mom let my aunt name my new baby sister.
Girl: What did she name her?
Boy: Denise.

STUPID FAIRY TALES

Did you hear about the **Big Bad Wolf** who invested in dynamite? He wanted to blow the **Three Little Pigs'** house away this time.

Did you hear about the princess who did everything wrong? She once kissed a prince and turned him into a frog.

Have you ever read the fairy tale about Tom Thumb's baby brother Pinky?

They updated Beauty and the Beast. Now at the end of the story they visit an Ikea.

Cinderella wised up. She went to the ball wearing an alarm clock around her neck so she wouldn't forget when to leave.

Rapunzel didn't let down her long hair to escape from the tall tower she was trapped in. She used a parachute instead.

Then there was the story of the lazy grasshopper that watched the busy ant work all summer. When the weather got cold, the grasshopper flew to Florida.

Did you hear Peter Pan was kicked out of flight school?
He could never land.

Did you hear Elsa was arrested for fraud?
They froze all her assets.

The Little Mermaid loves to go fish bowling.

CHAPTER

NIFTY KNOCK-KNOCKS

Knock! Knock!
Who's there?
Myah.
Myah who?
Myah mother told me to come over here.

Knock! Knock!
Who's there?
Slater.
Slater who?
Slater alligator.

Knock! Knock!
Who's there?
Seldom.
Seldom who?
I'm here to seldom cookies.

Knock! Knock!
Who's there?
Eve N.
Eve N. who?
Eve N. Steven.

Knock! Knock!
Who's there?
Weight.
Weight who?
Weight a minute and I'll tell you.

Knock! Knock!
Who's there?
Russ T. Potts.
Russ T. Potts who?
Russ T. Potts make food taste bad.

Knock! Knock!
Who's there?
Marsha.
Marsha who?
Marsha mellow.

Knock! Knock!
Who's there?
Andy.
Andy who?
Andy man special today.
Do you need anything fixed?

Knock! Knock!
Who's there?
Glow.
Glow who?
Glow ahead punk. Make my day.

Knock! Knock!
Who's there?
Ima.
Ima who?
Ima coming in, are you decent?

Knock! Knock!
Who's there?
Polk.
Polk who?
Polk your head out and take a look.

Knock! Knock!
Who's there?
Euro.
Euro who?
Eurolder than you sound.

Knock! Knock!
Who's there?
Alaya.
Alaya who?
Alaya friends are here, let us in!

Knock! Knock!
Who's there?
Scott.
Scott who?
Scott to be 10 degrees outside, open the door!

Knock! Knock!
Who's there?
Mums.
Mums who?
Mums the word, so be quiet.

SHHHH!

Knock! Knock!
Who's there?
Nick.
Nick who?
Nick tie.

Knock! Knock!
Who's there?
Duncan.
Duncan who?
Duncan doughnuts can be sloppy work.

Knock! Knock!
Who's there?
Handel.
Handel who?
Handel this problem for me.

Knock! Knock!
Who's there?
Hoffa.
Hoffa who?
Hoffa is it to the next gas station?

Knock! Knock!
Who's there?
Quint.
Quint who?
Quint fooling around and open the door.

Knock! Knock!
Who's there?
Folger.
Folger who?
Folger hands and sit quietly.

Knock! Knock!
Who's there?
Daren.
Daren who?
Daren back again!

Knock! Knock!
Who's there?
Gary.
Gary who?
Gary, Indiana.

Knock! Knock!
Who's there?
Flinch.
Flinch who?
Flinch fries.

Knock! Knock!
Who's there?
Hugh Paine.
Hugh Paine who?
Hugh Paine in the neck.

TELL HIM I SAID "THANKS"!

Knock! Knock!
Who's there?
I Otis.
I Otis who?
I Otis dollar to your father.

Knock! Knock!
Who's there?
Sara.
Sara who?
Sara Bellum.

Knock! Knock!
Who's there?
Mark.
Mark who?
Mark this date on your calendar.

Knock! Knock!
Who's there?
Abby.
Abby who?
Abby is trying to sting me, let me in!

Knock! Knock!
Who's there?
Athena.
Athena who?
I know Athena two about doors!

Knock! Knock!
Who's there?
Harve.
Harve who?
Harve your tickets ready.

Knock! Knock!
Who's there?
Nicholas.
Nicholas who?
Nicholas, penniless, and broke.

Knock! Knock!
Who's there?
Hester.
Hester who?
Hester any refreshments in there?

Knock! Knock!
Who's there?
Bias.
Bias who?
Bias a new TV, please.

Knock! Knock!
Who's there?
Sandy.
Sandy who?
Sandy package through FedEx.

Knock! Knock!
Who's there?
Distress.
Distress who?
Distress is too short. I'll wear a skirt instead.

Knock! Knock!
Who's there?
Ty.
Ty who?
Typhoon.

Knock! Knock!
Who's there?
O. Leo.
O. Leo who?
O. Leo Leahy.

Knock! Knock!
Who's there?
Chair.
Chair who?
Chair with those around you.

Knock! Knock!
Who's there?
Trains.
Trains who?
Trains-formers are crafty robots.

Knock! Knock!
Who's there?
I lecture.
I lecture who?
I lecture dog out when I came in.

Knock! Knock!
Who's there?
Adeline.
Adeline who?
Adeline and your essay will be complete.

Knock! Knock!
Who's there?
Thea Laura.
Thea Laura who?
Thea Laura inertia.

Knock! Knock!
Who's there?
Tattle.
Tattle who?
Tattle be the day when I tell you.

Knock! Knock!
Who's there?
Burton.
Burton who?
Burton up your shirt.

Knock! Knock!
Who's there?
Zita.
Zita who?
Zita moon coming up? It's getting late.

Knock! Knock!
Who's there?
Hood.
Hood who?
Hood you care to let me in?

Knock! Knock!
Who's there?
Your maid.
Your maid who?
Your maid your bed, now sleep in it.

Knock! Knock!
Who's there?
Harpy.
Harpy who?
Harpy birthday to you!

Knock! Knock!
Who's there?
Clara.
Clara who?
Clara-bunga, dude!

Knock! Knock!
Who's there?
Cosmo.
Cosmo who?
Cosmo people are arriving every minute.

Knock! Knock!
Who's there?
I. Lois.
I. Lois who?
I. Lois my way. Can you help me?

Knock! Knock!
Who's there?
Vine.
Vine who?
Vine weather we're having isn't it?

Knock! Knock!
Who's there?
Abi C.
Abi C. who?
Abi C. d e f g.

Knock! Knock!
Who's there?
Booking.
Booking who?
I've been Booking all over for your house!

Knock! Knock!
Who's there?
Orwell.
Orwell who?
Orwell, I finally give up.

Knock! Knock!
Who's there?
Alas.
Alas who?
Alas in Wonderland.

Knock! Knock!
Who's there?
Auntie.
Auntie Who?
Auntie-histimine.

Knock! Knock!
Who's there?
Emotion.
Emotion who?
An object emotion stays emotion.

Knock! Knock!
Who's there?
Hula.
Hula who?
Hula-la! It's a beautiful day.

Knock! Knock!
Who's there?
Muffin.
Muffin who?
Muffin ventured, muffin gained.

Knock! Knock!
Who's there?
Stirrup.
Stirrup who?
Stirrup the lemonade.

Knock! Knock!
Who's there?
Bizet.
Bizet who?
Bizet me at my house next weekend.

Knock! Knock!
Who's there?
Peace.
Peace who?
Peace open the door.

Knock! Knock!
Who's there?
Hut.
Hut who?
Hut diggity dog!

Knock! Knock!
Who's there?
Franz.
Franz who?
Franz is where you'll find the city of Paris.

Knock! Knock!
Who's there?
It's Max.
It's Max who?
It's Max no difference to me.

Knock! Knock!
Who's there?
Frame.
Frame who?
Frame and fortune await on your doorstep.

Knock! Knock!
Who's there?
Pig.
Pig who?
Pig me up at two o'clock.

Knock! Knock!
Who's there?
Attila.
Attila who?
Attila you open the door, I'm staying right here.

Knock! Knock!
Who's there?
Howe.
Howe who?
Howe do ma'am.

Knock! Knock!
Who's there?
Hits.
Hits who?
Hits later than you think.

Knock! Knock!
Who's there?
Carl Gogh.
Carl Gogh who?
Carl Gogh fast when you step on the gas.

Knock! Knock!
Who's there?
Marie.
Marie who?
Marie thon.

Knock! Knock!
Who's there?
Shell.
Shell who?
Shell we dance?

Knock! Knock!
Who's there?
Baggins.
Baggins who?
I'm Baggins to be let in!

Knock! Knock!
Who's there?
Merry.
Merry who?
Merry Poppins.

Knock! Knock!
Who's there?
Hiam.
Hiam who?
Hiam here for a visit.

Knock! Knock!
Who's there?
Sock.
Sock who?
Sock stalling and open the door!

Knock! Knock!
Who's there?
Hardy.
Hardy who?
Hardy har har! The joke is over. Let us in.

Knock! Knock!
Who's there?
Nobel.
Nobel who?
Nobel so I knocked instead.

Knock! Knock!
Who's there?
Dee.
Dee who?
Dee heck with you! I'm leaving.

Knock! Knock!
Who's there?
Whirl.
Whirl who?
Whirl try again later.

Knock! Knock!
Who's there?
Relent.
Relent who?
I relent the movie you borrowed from me.

Knock! Knock!
Who's there?
Ali.
Ali who?
Ali bama is a fine state.

Knock! Knock!
Who's there?
Atom.
Atom who?
Atom and Eve.

Knock! Knock!
Who's there?
Bruno.
Bruno who?
Bruno me. I live next door.

Knock! Knock!
Who's there?
Dot Burnett.
Dot Burnett who?
Dot Burnett I'm tired of this dumb game.

Knock! Knock!
Who's there?
Dairy.
Dairy who?
Dairy goes!
After him!

Knock! Knock!
Who's there?
Skipper.
Skipper who?
A Skipper keeps your coat closed.

· ·

Knock! Knock!
Who's there?
Almond.
Almond who?
Almond a very good mood.

· ·

Knock! Knock!
Who's there?
Wilda.
Wilda who?
Wilda plane be landing soon?

· ·

Knock! Knock!
Who's there?
Z.
Z who?
Z you in the morning.

· ·

Knock! Knock!
Who's there?
Olive.
Olive who?
Olive the spring, don't you.

Knock! Knock!
Who's there?
Jester.
Jester who?
Jester minute.
I'm still thinking.

· ·

Knock! Knock!
Who's there?
Rock it.
Rock it who?
Rock it ships fly into space.

· ·

Knock! Knock!
Who's there?
Skip.
Skip who?
Skip it! I'll go next door.

Knock! Knock!
Who's there?
Christopher Columbus.
Christopher Columbus who?
Duh! Christopher Columbus, the explorer.

• • • • • • • • • • • • • • • • • •

Knock! Knock!
Who's there?
Kent.
Kent who?
Kent you see who I am?

• • • • • • • • • • • • • • • • • •

Knock! Knock!
Who's there?
Dawn.
Dawn who?
Dawn with the wind.

• • • • • • • • • • • • • • • • • •

Knock! Knock!
Who's there?
Knight.
Knight who?
Knight of you to finally answer the door!

• • • • • • • • • • • • • • • • • •

Knock! Knock!
Who's there?
Howard.
Howard who?
Howard you like to buy some magazines?

Knock! Knock!
Who's there?
Ernie.
Ernie who?
Ernie got scraped when she fell on the sidewalk.

• • • • • • • • • • • • • • • • • •

Knock! Knock!
Who's there?
Canopy.
Canopy who?
Canopy ever grow up to be a string bean?

• • • • • • • • • • • • • • • • • •

Knock! Knock!
Who's there?
Ida.
Ida who?
Ida know.

• • • • • • • • • • • • • • • • • •

Knock! Knock!
Who's there?
Wilder.
Wilder who?
Wilder out let's order pizza.

• • • • • • • • • • • • • • • • • •

Knock! Knock!
Who's there?
Ozzie.
Ozzie who?
Ozzie a bad moon rising.

Knock! Knock!
Who's there?
Osborne.
Osborne who?
Osborne on the
4th of July.

***

Knock! Knock!
Who's there?
Winnie.
Winnie who?
Winnie gets home, he's in
for a big surprise.

***

Knock! Knock!
Who's there?
Nelda.
Nelda who?
Nelda bell doesn't work either.

Knock! Knock!
Who's there?
Oil.
Oil who?
Oil paint your picture if
you'll pose for me.

***

Knock! Knock!
Who's there?
Dot com.
Dot com who?
Dot com outside, it's raining.

***

Knock! Knock!
Who's there?
Freeze.
Freeze who?
Freeze a jolly good fellow, which
nobody can deny.

***

Knock! Knock!
Who's there?
Hour.
Hour who?
Hour you feeling?

***

Knock! Knock!
Who's there?
Lattice tissue.
Lattice tissue who?
Lattice tissue of the news is here.

Knock! Knock!
Who's there?
Hubie.
Hubie who?
Hubie a good boy while
we're gone!

Knock! Knock!
Who's there?
Al.
Al who?
Al in favor, say aye!

Knock! Knock!
Who's there?
Yarn.
Yarn who?
Yarn, I'm tired, let me in!

Knock! Knock!
Who's there?
Snow.
Snow who?
No. Snow White and the Seven
Dwarfs.

Knock! Knock!
Who's there?
Closure.
Closure who?
Closure mouth and
open the door.

Knock! Knock!
Who's there?
Gwen.
Gwen who?
Gwen are you going
to open this door?

Knock! Knock!
Who's there?
Vicious.
Vicious who?
Vicious a fine howdy-do
for a visitor.

Knock! Knock!
Who's there?
Sine.
Sine who?
Sine here for your package.

Knock! Knock!
Who's there?
House.
House who?
House it going with you?

Knock! Knock!
Who's there?
Althea.
Althea who?
Althea later, dude.

Knock! Knock!
Who's there?
Rut.
Rut who?
Rut do you want me to say?

Knock! Knock!
Who's there?
Megan.
Megan who?
Megan dinner is a lot of work.

Knock! Knock!
Who's there?
Ride.
Ride who?
Ride you tell a fib about me?

Knock! Knock!
Who's there?
Will Hugh?
Will Hugh who?
Will Hugh marry me?

Knock! Knock!
Who's there?
Ham Bacon.
Ham Bacon who?
Ham Bacon you to let me in.

Knock! Knock!
Who's there?
Hand.
Hand who?
Hand here's another thing!

Knock! Knock!
Who's there?
Frail.
Frail who?
Frail, you deserve a promotion.

Knock! Knock!
Who's there?
Lassie.
Lassie who?
Lassie what's on TV.

Knock! Knock!
Who's there?
Toby.
Toby who?
Toby or not Toby, that is the question.

Knock! Knock!
Who's there?
Hygiene.
Hygiene who?
Hygiene! What's new with you, Jean?

Knock! Knock!
Who's there?
Marcella.
Marcella who?
Marcella is flooded.
Can I borrow a mop?

Knock! Knock!
Who's there?
Habit.
Habit who?
Habit you're afraid to open the door.

Knock! Knock!
Who's there?
Wagons.
Wagons who?
No, it's wagons ho!

Knock! Knock!
Who's there?
Mo.
Mo who?
Molasses is very sweet syrup.

Knock! Knock!
Who's there?
Maggie.
Maggie who?
Maggie doesn't fit in the lock.

CHAPTER 5

WACKY INVENTIONS

Pancakes that harden into Frisbees if you don't eat them.

Doorbells that only work if someone you really want to see is at your front door.

Pants with lead-lined cuffs to keep people who are full of hot air from floating away.

A special clock that runs extra fast during school and work days and extra slow during vacations and weekends.

Real Christmas trees that never dry up and can be used year after year.

Robot babysitters that can be activated on a minute's notice, so parents never have to hunt for one in an emergency.

Refillable ice cream cones.

A cookbook that reads its recipes to you as you prepare the dish.

Kids shoes that grow at the same speed kids' feet grow.

Giant wetsuits for chilly hippos.

Murder mystery novels that have the last chapter first for people who can't wait to find out who did it.

A flyswatter tennis racket, so you can practice your swing and whack annoying insects at the same time.

Headlights for deer so car drivers can see them better at night.

Floating schoolbooks you don't have to carry in a backpack.

Huge bird baths for ostriches.

A basketball that dribbles itself for clumsy athletes who like to play hoops.

Hot air conditioners for cold, winter nights.

A car that can turn into a mini-helicopter in traffic jams.

Doggie bags for ice cream sundaes you can't finish.

A mirror that shows the reflection of a beautiful person no matter who looks into it.

Balsa wood bricks for karate experts who want to break things but have delicate hands.

Shoes that automatically change into slippers when you come home from work.

A cookie jar that magically refills itself when treats get low.

Doughnuts with handles for people who like to dunk but want to keep their fingers dry.

Sturdy chips you can easily chew, but never snap off in the dip.

Sprinkler flowerpots that automatically turn on to water your houseplants when they need moisture.

An escalator stepladder that you don't have to climb, which stops at a predetermined height.

A transparent refrigerator for people who want to watch what they eat.

An emotion elevator to raise your happiness levels.

A perfume that drives rich bankers wild. It smells like freshly minted money.

Neon thumbs that glow for people forced to hitchhike on dark highways at night.

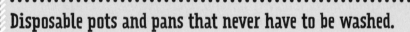

A comfortable reclining bicycle seat.

An alarm calendar that rings on relatives' and friends' birthdays so you never forget to buy a gift.

Disposable pots and pans that never have to be washed.

A boomerang baseball that returns to you after you throw it so you can play catch alone.

Eyeglasses with tiny watches in the frames for clock-watchers.

A bicycle that can go forward or backward.

High heel sneakers for people who want to look fashionable while jogging.

A spray that makes your skin so tough that bees, mosquitoes, and other stinging insects can't bite through it.

Traffic lights for wild animals so they can cross busy streets.

A bicycle that automatically pedals itself up steep hills while the rider rests.

Pancakes that automatically flip themselves when they're done on one side.

Bait worms that squeak like mice to attract catfish.

A rollerblade chair for people who are too tired to skate standing up.

Electric rocking chairs that rock when you plug them in for kids with short legs.

Knick-knacks that repel dust.

Kites with wings that flap so you can fly them when there's no wind.

Grass toupees for bald spots in the front lawn.

▶ ▶ ▶ ▶ ▶ ▶ ▶ ▶ ▶ ▶ ▶ ▶

A backyard birdie shower for birds who don't like to take baths.

◀ ◀ ◀ ◀ ◀ ◀ ◀ ◀ ◀ ◀ ◀ ◀

A dentist drill that plays sweet music instead of making an awful sound.

▶ ▶ ▶ ▶ ▶ ▶ ▶ ▶ ▶ ▶ ▶ ▶

Tree leaves that explode into mulch when they hit the ground. You don't have to rake them and they feed the grass.

◀ ◀ ◀ ◀ ◀ ◀ ◀ ◀ ◀ ◀ ◀ ◀ ◀ ◀ ◀ ◀ ◀ ◀

Doughnuts with no holes so you get more bites for your money.

▶ ▶ ▶ ▶ ▶ ▶ ▶ ▶ ▶ ▶ ▶ ▶ ▶ ▶ ▶ ▶ ▶ ▶ ▶

Suitcases with beeper signals that make them easy to locate at an airport.

◀ ◀ ◀ ◀ ◀ ◀ ◀ ◀ ◀ ◀ ◀ ◀ ◀ ◀ ◀ ◀ ◀ ◀

Animal bridges over busy country roads for deer, turtles, and other creatures.

▶ ▶ ▶ ▶ ▶ ▶ ▶ ▶ ▶ ▶ ▶ ▶ ▶ ▶ ▶ ▶

A people vacuum for kids who don't like showers or baths.

◀ ◀ ◀ ◀ ◀ ◀ ◀ ◀ ◀ ◀ ◀ ◀ ◀ ◀ ◀ ◀

A T-bone steak with an edible bone so there's less waste.

A Congressional Ordinary Medal, which can be awarded to folks who never do anything heroic or special, so they can feel important, too.

▶ ▶ ▶ ▶ ▶ ▶ ▶ ▶ ▶ ▶ ▶ ▶ ▶

Dog collars with headphones for pets who like to listen to music while being walked.

◀ ◀ ◀ ◀ ◀ ◀ ◀ ◀ ◀ ◀ ◀

Pancakes that have maple syrup mixed into the batter to save time at the breakfast table.

▶ ▶ ▶ ▶ ▶ ▶ ▶ ▶ ▶ ▶ ▶ ▶ ▶ ▶ ▶ ▶ ▶ ▶

A phone that comes up with wise answers to insults during an argument.

◀ ◀ ◀ ◀ ◀ ◀ ◀ ◀ ◀ ◀ ◀ ◀ ◀ ◀ ◀ ◀

A car that runs on pollutants instead of producing them.

▶ ▶ ▶ ▶ ▶ ▶ ▶ ▶ ▶ ▶ ▶ ▶ ▶ ▶ ▶ ▶

Polos for dogs complete with flea collars.

◀ ◀ ◀ ◀ ◀ ◀ ◀ ◀ ◀ ◀ ◀ ◀ ◀ ◀ ◀ ◀

Floating golf balls for golfers plagued by the water hazard.

▶ ▶ ▶ ▶ ▶ ▶ ▶ ▶ ▶ ▶ ▶ ▶ ▶ ▶ ▶

A combination basketball court and trampoline so everyone can dunk the ball.

Nerf dumbbells for kids who want to lift weights.

Pockets with combination locks to discourage pickpockets.

Automatic neckties that tie themselves around your neck.

Pizza-flavored bubblegum.

A Venus flytrap plant that gobbles up dust particles so you never have to dust your house.

Fruits with edible skins so you don't have to peel them.

Butter glue that sticks to corn on the cob.

Preheated soup that comes out of the can warm for hungry folks who can't wait to eat.

Super smart sheep that knit their own wool into clothing so you can cut out the middleman.

Air-conditioned hats
for hotheads.

Rainproof, domed parks so picnics and barbeques will never again be washed out.

Air-cooled sidewalks so the pavement never gets too hot during the summer.

Rowboats with motorized oars that work by themselves when you get tired.

Interactive television shows that allow you to debate the host or question guests from the privacy of your own home.

Report cards that automatically self-destruct if a student gets bad grades.

Books that are totally condensed into a foreword and an epilogue for people who have limited time to read.

Money that sticks to your fingers so it's harder to spend and easier to hold onto.

A joke book that contains canned laughter so you don't have to chuckle alone as you read it.

Tiny capsules that grow into artificial flowers when you plant them in your garden.

Pillows stuffed with cotton candy for folks who crave a sweet snack in the middle of the night.

A stabilizer kit for shaky excuses.

A hair blower that dries your hair and also combs or styles it at the same time.

Miniature cabanas attached to trees and shrubs that lazy caterpillars can use to turn into butterflies.

Wristwatches with tiny alarms that sound off if you have bad breath.

A bowling ball made out of foam for little kids.

A remote-controlled bowling ball for lazy athletes.

Special miniature brainwave recorders that print out your thoughts for people who always forget what they were going to say.

Robot shoes programmed to perform any dance in the world, so people never have to master any steps on their own.

Special tape you can use to mend rips or tears in clothing for people who don't know how to sew.

Underwater rocking chairs for senior citizen mermaids.

Hovercraft blue jeans for people who want to crowd surf during rock concerts.

Miniature working vacuums for dollhouses.

A showerhead that plays music as water streams out so you can sing your favorite songs as you scrub yourself.

Large trees with Swiss-cheese-type holes so telephone wires can pass through and the trees don't have to be cut down.

Toupees that actually grow on their own so bald people can enjoy getting a haircut.

Houses with mechanical robot arms so they can paint themselves.

Maple trees with special faucets that grow out of their trunks.

Gift-wrapped empty boxes to give to people who never want you to give them anything.

A bed with a built-in catapult that shoots you out of bed when the alarm goes off.

A TV set that automatically shuts itself off and on before and after commercials.

Galoshes with holes in them for kids who promise to wear rain boots, but love to get their feet wet.

Clothes with adjustable sizes you can still wear if you lose or gain weight.

A mirror that makes you look good early in the morning.

A bed with robot arms that makes itself.

Special satellite lighthouses in the sky so birds won't get lost in the fog when they migrate.

A bathroom scale with no numbers on it for people with low self-esteem.

A fork that bends if you put too much food on it.

An exercise bike that helps generate electricity for your house or apartment to keep you fit and save you money.

Special peel-off bark that can be made into paper products so trees never have to be cut down.

Nails that automatically drill themselves into wood so you never hit your thumb with a hammer.

Giant parachutes for airliners so there will never be any plane crashes.

Miniature bathing suits for shy goldfish.

Toupees that naturally turn gray so you don't have to buy a new one.

Moving sidewalks in school halls so students never have to run to their next class.

Frisbee plates you can eat off of and play with at picnics and at the beach.

CHAPTER 6

FUNNY THINGS

What happened when the sink and the bathtub started an advertising campaign?
They plugged themselves.

What did the clothesline say to the wet laundry?
You're really dampening the mood.

What did one speaker system say to the other?
I have some sound advice for you.

Why did the parked clock get a ticket?
It was over the time limit.

What did the nose say to the index finger?
Stop picking on me.

What's the best way to ship someone a toupee?
Send it via hairmail.

What did the guitar say to the rock musicians?
Pick me.

Why was the arrow so angry?
It was fired from a crossbow.

Why did the mattress go to the doctor?
It had spring fever.

What does a novel wear to keep warm?
A dust jacket.

Man: Does your wristwatch keep accurate time?
Jogger: No, it runs fast.

What do you get when a phone wears a shirt?
A ring around the collar.

What did the
broken clock say?
Will someone please
give me a hand?

Why was the letter
delivered in the morning
all wet?
It had postage dew.

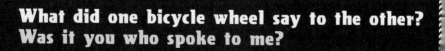

What did one bicycle wheel say to the other?
Was it you who spoke to me?

Kenny: Have you ever heard of broom fever?
Jenny: No. What is it?
Kenny: It's an epidemic that's sweeping across the country.

When do old clocks pass away?
When their number is up.

What did one helicopter say to the other?
Drop by my pad later today.

What did the sharpener say to the pencil?
You can leave now. You've made your point.

What did the sword say to the angry saber?
Don't get all bent out of shape.

Publisher: Is this book about blankets any good?
Editor: It's just another cover story.

Why did the broken chair lose an argument?
It didn't have a leg to stand on.

What do you get if you cross the ocean and a cartoon duck?
Salt Water Daffy.

What kind of dots dance?
Polka dots.

What did the clothesline say to the clean laundry?
Hey guys! Hang around with me for a while.

What language do clocks speak?
Tick talk.

What did the old lawn chair say to the new lawn chair?
Welcome to the fold.

What did one lounge chair say to encourage the other lounge chair?
Just **put** one **futon** front of the other.

What did the gas oven say to the furnace?
You've really got me fuming.

What did one cemetery say to the other?
Are you plotting against me?

Jenny: **Did you hear the rumor about the burning building?**
Penny: **No. Is it hot gossip?**

Why did the trumpet take an algebra class?
It wanted to be a math tooter.

How do you lock up a motel?
Use a hotel chain.

What do you get if you cross a diaper and a handbag?
A change purse.

What did the cowboy say to the tangled lasso?
That's knot funny.

What should you do if your clothes keep getting wet?
Dry harder.

Did you hear about the entertainment center that wouldn't sit down? It was a TV stand.

Why did the reading glasses hate traveling?
They weren't good with distance.

What do you get from a zombie furnace?
A dead heat.

SIGN IN DRY CLEANERS: We've got it in the bag.

. . . .

What did the fast car say to the sharp curve?
It was an honor to swerve you.

. . . .

What do you get when you cross a purse with a dark room?
I don't know, but you'll never find anything in there!

. . . .

Why are rich Englishmen so strong?
All their money is measured in pounds.

. . . .

What did the ceiling say to the chandelier?
You're the only bright spot in my life.

. . . .

Why did the playing card become a ship?
It wanted to be a full deck.

. . . .

Hal: What do you call a boomerang that doesn't work?
Val: A stick.

A man built a car totally out of wood. It had wooden seats, a wooden body and wooden wheels. It even had a wooden engine. There was only one big problem with his invention: the car wooden go.

▶ ▶ ▶ ▶ ▶ ▶ ▶ ▶ ▶ ▶ ▶ ▶ ▶ ▶ ▶

What did the drumstick say to the drum?
I bet I can beat you in a race!

Who tells scary nursery rhymes?
Mother Goosebumps.

▶ ▶ ▶ ▶ ▶ ▶ ▶ ▶ ▶ ▶ ▶ ▶ ▶ ▶ ▶

Did you hear about the percussionist running for office?
He's working on drumming up support.

What did the drapes say to the decorator?
Don't sash me.

▶ ▶ ▶ ▶ ▶ ▶ ▶ ▶ ▶ ▶ ▶ ▶ ▶ ▶ ▶

What did the dying window shout?
It's curtains for me!

◀ ◀ ◀ ◀ ◀ ◀ ◀ ◀ ◀ ◀ ◀ ◀ ◀ ◀ ◀

Why was the window worried?

He thought he was going blind.

▶ ▶ ▶ ▶ ▶ ▶ ▶ ▶ ▶ ▶ ▶ ▶ ▶ ▶ ▶

What did the handyman say to the wall?
One more crack like that and I'll plaster you.

Son: *Hey, Dad! You know that black box that always survives plane crashes?*
Father: *Yes. What about it?*
Son: *Why don't they make the whole plane out of the same stuff?*

▶ ▶ ▶ ▶ ▶ ▶ ▶ ▶ ▶

What's Honest Abe's favorite kind of car?
A Lincoln.

◀ ◀ ◀ ◀ ◀ ◀ ◀ ◀

ACME TOYS: Our life's work is child's play.

▶ ▶ ▶ ▶ ▶ ▶ ▶ ▶ ▶ ▶ ▶ ▶ ▶ ▶ ▶

Why did the parachute school close?
It had too many dropouts.

▷ ▷ ▷ ▷ ▷ ▷ ▷ ▷ ▷ ▷

What did the composer do when he got mad he couldn't open his door?
He flew off the Handel.

▶ ▶ ▶ ▶ ▶ ▶ ▶ ▶ ▶ ▶ ▶ ▶ ▶ ▶

What did Mr. Candle say to Ms. Candle?

Are you going out tonight?

Anne: Do you want some parting advice?
Dan: Sure.
Anne: Look in a mirror when combing your hair.

Why did the little boy pull
the plug on the bathtub?
He wanted to go
for a drain ride.

What does Santa call where he lives?
His ho-ho-home.

Why was the sink so tired?
It was feeling drained.

SILLY SLOGANS:
ACME WELL DIGGERS: We're in the hole sale business.
ACME AIR CONDITIONED PLANE HANGERS: We cool your jets.

Why did the bulletin board quit his job?
He just couldn't tack it anymore.

Reporter: I had to leave that new play early.
Did it have a happy ending?
Critic: We were all happy when it was over.

NOTICE: A tailor can make torn pants seam
right again.

TONGUE TWISTERS:
She sawed six slick, sleek, slim, slender saplings.
The sun shines on the shop signs.
Six sick soldiers sighted seven slowly sinking ships.

What college did Mr. Clock graduate from?
Georgia Tick.

What did the hole say to the trench?
Let's ditch your friend.

What did one cabinet say to the other?
Help your shelf.

Why did the shoe say ouch?
It bit its tongue.

Why are everybody's pants too short?
Because their legs always stick out two feet.

Why did the wheel get an education?
Because it wanted to be well-rounded.

Cowgirl: Do you want to hear a joke about a cattle roundup?
Cowboy: No thanks. When you've herd one, you've herd them all.

Which state is the trouser state?
Pantsylvania.

Zeb: My new scarecrow is so ugly it scared away every crow for miles.

Jeb: Well my new scarecrow is so ugly it scared our crows into bringing back the corn they stole last year.

Which state is very cold in the winter?
Burrmont.

Which state is kind of sloppy?
Messachusetts.

Which state has the most highways?
Road Island.

What do you get if you cross a traffic light and a bonfire?
Smoke signals.

What is full of holes but still holds water?
A sponge.

What did the lasso say to the steer that escaped?
I guess you're not in the loop anymore.

Why did the thermometer go to college?
It wanted a higher degree.

Where do Mack trucks go to have fun?
To a trailer park.

Why are kittens bad at jokes?
They take everything litterally.

Where does a train go to work out?
To a jogging track.

What kind of trousers does a new conductor wear?
Training pants.

What did the highway construction boss say as he climbed a hill?
I guess we'll have to upgrade our plans for this road.

House Hunter: Does this home have a finished basement?
Real Estate Agent: Yes. In fact, it's ranked number-one on our best cellar list.

Why was the little radio sad?
His mother wouldn't let him play outside.

SILLY SLOGANS:

ACME FOOTWEAR: Try our shoes and you'll be happy to put your foot down.

ACME BED & BREAKFAST: The Inn Crowd loves us.

ACME HUMIDIFIERS: You can't dew without our product.

ACME SURVEILLANCE: Not on our watch.

ACME CLOTHESPINS: We produce top-of-the-line products.

ATTENTION:
Grammar instructors always mark your words.

ATTENTION: Glue and paste now on sale. Low sticker prices.

ATTENTION: Dentist bills can take a big bite out of your paycheck.

ATTENTION: Friendly pigs make swine friends.

ATTENTION: Army barbers know all the short cuts.

What did the cart say to the shopper?
Quit pushing me around.

What do you get if you cross the Green Giant and a pool table?
A peashooter.

Jack: How did you repair that broken grandfather clock?
Mack: I used ticker tape.

What do you get if you kiss glue?
Lip stick.

What do you get if you cross a water spring with a ballpoint?
A fountain pen.

What do you get if you cross cotton with detergent?
Soft soap.

Did you hear about the farmer who crossed a sewing machine with a tractor and got a vehicle that sews seeds?

What's the easiest way to hold your breath?
Blow it into a balloon.

SILLY SAIDS:
"I'm lost," Tom cried remotely.
"I loved the Valentine you sent me," sighed Tom heartily.

What's the best way to tear up a Valentine card?
Half-heartedly.

What do you call an exact duplicate of Texas?
The Clone Star State.

WANT ODDS:
Drama school needs acting principal.
Car repair shop needs motor head.
Bodybuilder needs new muscle car.
Math department needs add expert.

"This new robot will do half of your work," the salesman promised the hard-working, self-employed man. "That's marvelous," said the potential buyer. "In that case, I'll take two."

The furniture department needed to have a conference. "Who'll come to the meeting?" asked the sofa. "I'll come and shed some light on our problem areas," said the lamp. "You can count on me," said the table. "All we need now," said the sofa, "is someone to chair our committee."

KOOKY QUESTIONS:
Are tailors sewer workers?

Why did the tightrope walker quit the circus?
He finally reached the end of his rope.

What do you find on the ogre turnpike?
Troll booths.

What word is always pronounced badly?
Badly.

Why did the chef put a clock in a hot pan?
He wanted to see time fry.

What do you take when you're going from your old house to your new house?
Moving pictures.

Ted: You should never write a love letter on an empty stomach.
Fred: Why not?
Ted: Paper is better.

Where does one find an ocean with no water?
On a map.

ATTENTION: Pillow Company needs workers looking for a soft job.

Why did the window answer the cell phone?
It was a curtain call.

What happened when the cruise ship *Red* crashed into the steamship *Blue* at sea?
All of the passengers were marooned.

What goes up and down but doesn't move?
A staircase.

Where can you find polluted belts?
Around toxic waists.

What did the hill say to Mount Rushmore?
I remember you when you
were two-faced.

Where did the sick tugboat go?
To the nearest dock.

Billionaire: Thanks for building this elegant estate for my family.
Contractor: Don't mansion it.

Where did the U.S. president live in prehistoric times?
Washington, B.C.E.

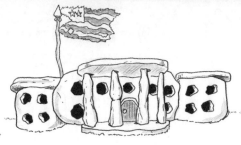

 1600 PENNSTONEVANIA AVENUE

What kind of pants did the corn farmer wear?
Husky pants.

Clerk: Would you like to buy one of our mountain bikes, sir?
Customer: Perhaps! If the price isn't too steep.

What did the measles say to the chicken pox?
Don't do anything rash.

What kind of stories should you tell during a slow boat ride?
Ferry tales.

Fran: How's your coin purse? Still empty?
Anne: Yes, no change.

Where do planes wash up?
In a jet stream.

What's slime's favorite game?
Slimon says.

Why doesn't a steam locomotive like to sit down?
Because it has a tender behind.

What card game did the artist play?
Draw poker.

What do you get if you plant an orchard in Astroturf?
Artificial fruit.

What do you get if you cross a pot of glue and a croquet set?
A sticky wicket.

How do you brighten up a dull garden?
With a light bulb.

When is a card game not tame?
When the deuces are wild.

Which card in the deck is helpful if you have a flat tire?
The Jack.

Why did the poker player run to the bathroom?
He had a flush.

What do you call a pair of dull scissors?
Two butter knives.

▶ ▶ ▶ ▶ ▶ ▶ ▶ ▶ ▶ ▶ ▶ ▶ ▶ ▶ ▶ ▶ ▶ ▶ ▶

Did you hear about the mouse who hated giving speeches?
Sounds like a cat got his tongue.

▶ ▶ ▶ ▶ ▶ ▶ ▶ ▶ ▶ ▶ ▶ ▶ ▶ ▶ ▶ ▶ ▶ ▶ ▶

What did the father broom say to baby broom?
It's time to go to sweep.

▶ ▶ ▶ ▶ ▶ ▶ ▶ ▶ ▶ ▶ ▶ ▶ ▶ ▶ ▶ ▶ ▶ ▶ ▶

NOTICE: Stones for sale at rock bottom prices!

WHAT DO YOU CALL . . .

...A boy named Richard covered in glue?
A sticky Ricky.

...A small child with a fever?
A hot tot.

...A father who is always patting folks on the back?
A slap-happy pappy.

...A story told in a stable?
A barn yarn.

...A jester who likes to play billiards?
A pool fool.

What did the doctor say to the feather mattress before telling him bad news?
You may want to lie down for this.

What do you call when a feline has a flat tire?
A cat tower.

Did you hear about the soccer comedy show?
People seemed to get a kick out of it.

Why does the president cover his eyes when he walks through his kitchen?
He wants to avoid another cabinet meeting.

What did the mop say when the broom bought it a present?
Aw, that's so sweep!

And then there was the sick light switch that didn't know when he was well off.

Trumpet: **Do you like being bagpipes?**
Bagpipes: **Yes. I'm proud to be a windbag.**

ATTENTION: Buy speakers for your big screen TV. They're a sound investment.

What did the hand say to the arm?
How about giving me a raise?

◄ ◄

What did the college mattress look forward to?
Spring Break.

► ►

ATTENTION: **A big grandfather clock is a long timer.**

◄ ◄

How do you dial a cell phone?
Use your ring finger.

► ►

What do you call an old piece of insect furniture?
An antique.

◄ ◄ ◄ ◄ ◄ ◄ ◄ ◄ ◄ ◄ ◄ ◄ ◄ ◄ ◄ ◄ ◄ ◄ ◄ ◄

Why can't you find any brooms in New York?
It's the city that never sweeps.

► ►

How much wood can a computer chop?
A cord or two.

◄ ◄

Why was the wooden chair so unpopular?
It had a warped sense of pride.

► ►

What do you call a very young cannon?
A baby boomer.

What did the little pebbles go down at the playground?
The rock slide.

ATTENTION: Stonehenge is a rock hall of fame.

TONGUE TWISTERS:
"Swim, Sally," slim Sam shouted shyly.
"Bye, Bye, Bluebird," Billy Beaver bellowed.
Lucky Louie Lion likes licking lemon lollipops.
Friendly Freda Fly flips flapjacks.

What's the best way to pass a geometry exam?
Figure out all the angles.

Did you hear about the toilet who got married?
I can't wait to meet the flushing bride.

Did you hear about the pessimistic hourglass?
It was a glass half empty kind of person.

What happens when the sun is happy?
It beams with joy.

What is the favorite cartoon of little drums?
Tom-tom and Jerry.

How do you write to a deep hole for mining minerals?
Send a quarry letter.

Where does rich slime live?
On Oozy Street.

What city was the capital of the ancient corn civilization?
Cornstantinople.

CRAZY QUESTION:
Are prisoners' suits jailor-made?

MADE WITH PRIDE IN CELL BLOCK D-331

Ms. Bracelet: **Why are you so exhausted?**
Mr. Clock: **I've been running the whole day.**

Lady: Do cruise ships like this one sink very often?
Sailor: No, ma'am. Only once.

What do you find at the foot of the turnpike?
A toe booth.

How do trumpets keep away thieves?
With a bugler alarm.

What do you get if you cross a trampoline and pop music?
A song that jumps up the charts.

Where can you buy a vintage Volkswagen?
Try an Old Volks Home.

KOOKY QUESTION: Does a sword swallower have a razor-sharp tongue?

Man: I'd like to buy a round trip ticket.
Bus Depot Clerk: Where to?
Man: Duh! Back to here.

Woman: Can I get a ticket for Madison?
Ticket Clerk: Where is Madison?
Woman: He's the little boy standing by the vending machines.

Did you hear about the fake hair that was really upset?
It really wigged out.

Judge: Tell the truth, Mr. James. Were you and Mr. Smith having a fistfight?

Mr. Jones: No, your honor.

Mr. Smith: Yes, your honor.

Mr. Jones: Don't believe him, judge. He's still punchy.

What do you get when you cross a mop and a basketball player?
Someone who can wipe the floor with the competition.

Did you hear about the ship full of violins?
It was a boatload of treble.

What do you get if you cross a watch with a politician running for election?
A clock with a hand that shakes.

Dora: Why do you have a piece of string tied around your finger?

Cora: My mom tied it to me. It's to remind me to mail a letter for her.

Dora: Did it work? Did you mail your mom's letter?

Cora: No. She forgot to give it to me.

What do you get when you cross a newspaper and a jalapeño pepper?
Something red hot off the press.

Why was Mr. Match so happy?
He was voted into the Hall of Flame.

Uncle Al: My alma mater was so small we didn't have a college choir. We had a college duet.

What did the black checker say to the red checker?
So long. I'm going to move.

Where does a chess board go when it needs money?
The pawn shop.

What did the price tag yell at the checkout counter?
Help! I've been ripped off.

SIGN IN A SPEECH CLASS: Don't be quiet.

What do you get if you cross a watch with a boxer?
A clock with fists instead of hands.

Where do rich surfers go to study?
Boarding school.

SIGN ON A POST OFFICE: We were the first to be letter-perfect.

SIGN IN ALASKA: Charity begins at Nome.

Why did the mittens get married?
They were in glove with each other.

What do you get if you cross a watch with a nice person?
A clock that's always willing to give you a hand.

What do you call a dishonest fairy?
A Leprecon.

How do you keep your house dry?
Don't pay the water bill.

Millie: What's a skeleton?
Billy: It's a person with the inside out and the outside off.

What do you call secretive instructions for opening a zipper?
A zip code.

What kind of dirt is lots of fun?
Playground.

What do you get if you cross the beach with bagpipes?
Sandpipers.

TONGUE TWISTED:
Round the rugged rocks the ragged rascal ran.
Green and gray geese gaily grazing in Greece.
Blue beaus pose with bows.
Surely the sun shall shine soon.
Windy weather makes Wendy Worm wiggle wildly.

Why are Medieval history books always so big?
They had a lot of pages.

What do traffic lights and clickbait articles have in common?
They both seem to be red a lot.

What did Ms. Clock say to her student wristwatches when the bell rang?
Please exit the class in a timely fashion.

ATTENTION: If you want a fresh holiday tree, do your Christmas chopping early.

What did the clock say at the board meeting?
I second that proposal.

Mr. Hour: Why did you name your little clock Tick?
Father Time: Because he doesn't tock much.

Jill: Have you ever seen
a barn dance?
Bill: No, but I've seen
a house party.

What did the wall say when someone put a push pin in it?
Stop a tacking me!

How do you make an apple go bananas?
You drive it out of its rind.

How do you catch a beach monster?
Use a sand trap.

What did the road say to the bridge?
You made me cross.

What color do you paint a piano?
Plink.

Where did the pianos vacation in Florida?
At Key Largo.

Bill: Did you hear the joke about the new airplane?

Jill: No.

Bill: Never mind. It'll probably go over your head.

What do you get if you cross a rundown shack and Saint Nicholas?
Shanty Claus.

Where do monster locomotives live?
In Trainsylvania.

Why did the chimney sweep go to a doctor?
He needed a flue shot.

How do you repair a broken joke?
Use slapstick humor.

ACME Air Conditioning: **A cool company.**

How does a dinosaur learn new words?
He uses a thesaurus.

Where do concrete blocks meet new friends?
At a cement mixer.

What's red and white and bumpy?
A snowman with acne.

What do you cal a coffee cup with no sense of fashion?
One ugly mug.

What do you get if you cross fossils and dishes?
Bone china.

My house is so cold, I just saw a penguin paying rent.

My house is so small, I just saw two ants fighting for closet space.

My house is so old, I ran into a dinosaur who used to live there.

My house is so smelly, I just had two skunks ask to move in.

My house is so haunted, Casper hired an exorcist.

Which piece of living room furniture plays football?
The end table.

What did the track official say to the dining room table?
Get set.

When should you wrap a TV show in a blanket?
When it has a cold open.

How do farmers know if there has been an earthquake?
The dairy barns are full of milk shakes.

▶ ▶ ▶ ▶ ▶ ▶ ▶ ▶ ▶ ▶

What's big and yellow and bad at hide and seek?
A school bus.

◀ ◀ ◀ ◀ ◀ ◀ ◀ ◀ ◀ ◀ ◀

Jill: Is the horn on your car broken?
Bill: No. It just doesn't give a hoot.

▶ ▶ ▶ ▶ ▶ ▶ ▶ ▶ ▶ ▶ ▶ ▶ ▶ ▶ ▶ ▶ ▶

What did the shovel say to the hole?
Let's get to the bottom of this.

◀ ◀ ◀ ◀ ◀ ◀ ◀ ◀ ◀ ◀ ◀ ◀ ◀ ◀ ◀ ◀ ◀ ◀ ◀

Why do pillows make fine lawyers?
They know a good case when they see it.

▶ ▶ ▶ ▶ ▶ ▶ ▶ ▶ ▶ ▶ ▶ ▶ ▶ ▶ ▶ ▶ ▶

Did you hear about the sweaters that did everything together?
They were a close knit group.

◀ ◀ ◀ ◀ ◀ ◀ ◀ ◀ ◀ ◀ ◀ ◀ ◀ ◀ ◀ ◀ ◀ ◀

Show me America's first pair of false teeth and I'll show you the George Washington bridge.

▶ ▶ ▶ ▶ ▶ ▶ ▶ ▶ ▶ ▶ ▶ ▶ ▶ ▶ ▶ ▶ ▶

How do you put a hearse in second gear?
Use the graveyard shift.

How did Noah see in the dark?
He put up ark lights.

▶ ▶ ▶ ▶ ▶ ▶ ▶ ▶ ▶ ▶ ▶ ▶ ▶ ▶ ▶ ▶ ▶ ▶

Where do cavemen go to party?
The club.

◀ ◀ ◀ ◀ ◀ ◀ ◀ ◀ ◀ ◀ ◀ ◀ ◀ ◀ ◀ ◀ ◀

**Why is a quarter smarter
than a dime?**
It has more cents.

▶ ▶ ▶ ▶ ▶ ▶ ▶ ▶ ▶ ▶ ▶

*What did the robot say to
the gas pump?*
*Take your finger out of
your ear and listen to me.*

◀ ◀ ◀ ◀ ◀ ◀ ◀ ◀ ◀ ◀ ◀ ◀ ◀ ◀ ◀ ◀ ◀ ◀

What is a trumpet's favorite day of the week?
Toots Day.

▶ ▶ ▶ ▶ ▶ ▶ ▶ ▶ ▶ ▶ ▶ ▶ ▶ ▶ ▶ ▶ ▶ ▶

Why should you never read books about witchcraft?
They're hex-rated.

◀ ◀ ◀ ◀ ◀ ◀ ◀ ◀ ◀ ◀ ◀ ◀ ◀ ◀ ◀ ◀ ◀

Why is the piano giggling?
Someone was tickling its keys.

▶ ▶ ▶ ▶ ▶ ▶ ▶ ▶ ▶ ▶ ▶ ▶ ▶ ▶ ▶ ▶ ▶ ▶

What do you need to fasten spy pants?
A zip code.

Where did the creek stream live?
On Facebrook.

Which vegetable won the hurdles event at the track meet?
The jumping bean.

Bill: Where can you buy a buck?
Jill: Go to a dollar store.

Bill: If I wash my face, will it be clean?
Jill: Let's soap for the best.

SILLY SAIDS:

"I paint and sculpt," Tom said artfully.

"I like making art projects at home," said Tom in a crafty way.

Why is an editor's desk always cold?
There are too many drafts.

Why did the clock buy spices?
He was out of thyme.

Why did the wood-burning stove join a fitness club?
It was turning into a pot-bellied stove.

What did the mother give her toddler?
A surprise potty.

How did the tornado win a medal for bravery?
It fought in Whirl War II.

What did the drill sergeant say to the rope?
Line up.

What did the drill sergeant say after the rope lined up?
Knot now!

What did the drill sergeant say to the rope after the wet laundry came out?
Soldier, your job is to keep them pinned down.

NOTICE: The Navy announced the cost of upgrading its submarines has tripled this year. Even the price of going down has gone up.

How do you fix a charley horse?
Go to a cramp counselor.

STUPID SENTENCES:

When you change Judy's diaper sprinkler with baby powder.

The gym teacher said Billy and I make quite a pear.

Absent a letter to my Aunt June.

The angry fruit magician made us dis a pear.

If your blankets are too short, your fiddlestick out.

Yes, we do currently have a room toilet.

The problem with the fast baseball player was no one could catcher.

Mr. Jones walks around with a stiff neck because he's afraid his wiggle fall off.

How do you handcuff a barber?
Use locks of hair.

Why did the crooked belt go to jail?
The judge suspended his sentence.

Why was the sponge fired?
He kept loufaing around.

What do you get if you cross a minister and an organ?
A prayer piano.

Which city in Nebraska is a real funny place?
Omaha-ha.

Jim: Which side of the cake is the right side?

Slim: I don't know.

Jim: The side that has been eaten because the other side is left.

What do you get if you cross a clock and a man who stepped on a small nail?
Tick tack toe.

Ken: Why did you move to Hawaii?
Jen: I wanted to spend my vacations at home and still enjoy myself.

Who speaks all the languages of the world?
An echo.

Why are showers always in trouble?
They're always in hot water.

What did Pinocchio say to the woodpecker?
Go away. I don't need another hole in my head.

Why was the clock crying?
A bully twisted its arm.

What did the old watch say to the digital clock?
The time business is getting out of hand.

UNSOLVED SILLY MYSTERIES

Dig a hole. Carefully pile the dirt you take out nearby. Now try to fill the same hole back up with the same dirt. You always end up with too much dirt or not enough.

The richest guy you know ends up winning a million dollars in the state lottery. The poorest guy you know wins a two-dollar cash prize.

The last piece of cheesecake magically disappears from the fridge and nobody admits taking it.

Fertilize, water, and pamper a plant you want to grow and it dies. Ignore a plant you don't care about and it grows and multiplies.

The guy who never bothers with his lawn has great grass. The guy who slaves over his lawn grows weeds.

When you barbecue, the cheap burgers turn out perfect and the expensive steak burns to a crisp.

The biggest and best piece of fruit always grows on the top of the tree far out of reach.

The kid who is too tired to do his homework has plenty of energy for video games.

All the best movies you're dying to see are on the day you have no time for TV. When you have all day to watch TV, only lousy movies are on.

The dude with a makeshift bamboo pole hooks a whopper, while the angler with expensive fishing gear reels in a minnow.

CHAPTER 7

THE DAFFY DICTIONARY

Acorn: An oak in a nutshell.

Acquaintance: A person you know well enough to borrow from but not well enough to lend to.

Actor: A person who works hard at being someone other than himself most of the time.

Adult: A person who has stopped growing at both ends and is now growing in the middle.

Air Force Pilots: Soldiers with their noses up in the air.

Alarm clock: A device to wake up people who don't have small children or pets that need to go out.

Antarctic: Snowman's land.

I COULD GO FOR PIZZA DELIVERY RIGHT NOW!

Antiques: Merchandise sold for old time's sake.

Archaeologist: Someone who keeps digging old things up.

Authorship: A writer's canoe.

Baby quadruplets: Four crying out loud.

Dentist: Proof that the tooth hurts.

Bad driver: The person your car rear-ended.

Balloon: Air today, gone tomorrow..

Bandstand: What a band has to do when someone takes away their chairs.

Baseball's Minor Leagues: The hope diamonds.

Basketball: A fancy dance for bugs held in a basket.

Big Belly Laugh: Girth quake.

Birth announcement: A stork quotation.

Blister: A heel's revenge for being stepped on.

Bore: A pig that's not very entertaining.

Bread: Raw toast.

Taxi Driver: Someone who gets in trouble for going the extra mile.

Bus Operator: A person who drives away even his best customers.

Business: When you don't have any of it, you go out of it.

Buzz saw: A honey of a woodcutter.

Camel: A horse with a speed bump.

Carp: A musical instrument played by angelfish in heaven.

Caterpillar: An upholstered worm.

Change purses: Old money bags.

Character: A thing few people have and a lot of people are.

Broke: Something that takes more money than you have to fix.

College: A place where a lot of wise guys hang out.

Thermostat: The higher it goes, the lower you feel.

ON STRIKE FOR MORE DOUGH!

Computer crash: When electronics byte the big one.

Cookout: A chef on strike.

Cottontail: A hoppy ending.

Cowardice: Cold water when it gets scared.

Manager: The only thing they manage is to get on your nerves.

Cricket: A game played by English grasshoppers.

Purse: Something that, the smaller it is, the more stuff you have in it.

Critic: A person who loves to hate plays and movies.

Declaration of Independence: A doctor's excuse that allows you to miss school for a week.

Dentist: A doctor with a lot of pull.

Sleep: The one thing you can never get enough of.

Diet: The victory of mind over platter.

Diplomacy: *Saying nice things to and doing nice things for people you really can't stand.*

Duck: A chicken with flat feet.

Dust: Mud with the juice squeezed out.

Egotist: An I-for-an-I kind of guy.

Patients: The more there are of them, the less of it you have.

Encore: Using flattery to get more than you paid for.

Eve: **Madam Adam.**

▶ ▶

Fast food: an oxymoron.

◀ ◀

On sale: Buy twice as much for half the guilt.

▶ ▶

Fish: A creature that goes on vacation the same time most fishermen do.

◀ ◀

Flagon: **A patriotic dragon.**

◀ ◀

Shoes: Something to ensure de feet.

◀ ◀

Restaurant: Where you pay more to eat less.

▶ ▶

Fresh water: You used to get it by turning on a tap, now you get it by twisting off a cap.

◀ ◀

Friend: A person who dislikes the same people you do and also has the same enemies.

▶ ▶

Funeral home: Where people are dying to get in.

◀ ◀

Garlic: Exercise food to make your breath strong.

▶ ▶

Geologist: A graduate of the School of Hard Knocks.

Gigantic: An antic performed by a wise guy giant.

▶ ▶ ▶ ▶ ▶ ▶ ▶ ▶ ▶ ▶ ▶ ▶

Glove: A sock you wear on your hand.

◀ ◀ ◀ ◀ ◀ ◀ ◀ ◀ ◀ ◀ ◀

*Good Manners: **The noises you don't make while eating or drinking.***

▶ ▶ ▶ ▶ ▶ ▶ ▶ ▶ ▶ ▶ ▶

Good sport: A foe that always lets you have the first pick when selecting teams.

◀ ◀ ◀ ◀ ◀ ◀ ◀ ◀ ◀ ◀

Grand Canyon: America's Hole of Fame.

▶ ▶ ▶ ▶ ▶ ▶ ▶ ▶ ▶ ▶ ▶ ▶ ▶ ▶

Granny Knot: What happens when Granny forgets to put her glasses on and ties her shoelaces.

◀ ◀ ◀ ◀ ◀ ◀ ◀ ◀ ◀ ◀ ◀ ◀

Gripe: A ripe grape.

▶ ▶ ▶ ▶ ▶ ▶ ▶ ▶ ▶ ▶ ▶ ▶

Hair: A dome covering.

◀ ◀ ◀ ◀ ◀ ◀ ◀ ◀ ◀ ◀ ◀ ◀ ◀ ◀ ◀

Halloween: Pranksgiving time.

Harmonica: Sweet chin music.

Hibernate: To live on burrowed time.

Hijack: A tool for changing tires on an airplane.

Honesty: The bitterest of drinks to swallow.

Horse sense: Stable thinking.

Hospital: Where the idea of visiting one is enough to make you sick.

Huddle: Athletes getting together to play some football.

Hug: People pulling together.

I COULDN'T HAVE DONE IT WITH- OUT YOU!

Raising a child: A teen building exercise.

Tailor: Someone always on pins and needles.

Icicle: An eavesdripper.

Icy path: **A slidewalk.**

Tower: *A high place to get your car stuck.*

Imitation: An invite to a party for a bunch of phonies.

ASAP: As soon as able to procrastinate.

Jar: A bottle with its mouth open wide.

Jelly: A nervous jam.

Work: **Something you'll spend your life trying to get away from.**

Jump: The last word in airplanes.

Elevator: They can raise you up or bring you down.

Kazoo: The sound of a loud sneeze.

Cactus: **A prickly personality.**

About Applesauce Press

Good ideas ripen with time. From seed to harvest,
Applesauce Press crafts books with beautiful designs,
creative formats, and kid-friendly information on a variety
of fascinating topics. Like our parent company, Cider Mill Press
Book Publishers, our press bears fruit twice a year,
publishing a new crop of titles each spring and fall.

Write to us at:
PO Box 454
12 Spring Street
Kennebunkport, ME 04046

Or visit us online at:
cidermillpress.com